What people are saying about …

Shrewd

"This book is flat-out brilliant! Ten pages in and my friends and I were already asking ourselves in meetings, 'How can we be shrewd in this situation?' I loved this book!"

Jon Acuff, *Wall Street Journal* best-selling
author of *Quitter* and *Stuff Christians Like*

"*Shrewd* is almost flawless. Rick Lawrence explores Jesus's mysterious command to be 'as wise as a serpent, as innocent as a dove' from every angle imaginable. From the opening exchange with the author's daughter to the last line of admonition—'live innocently shrewd'—you are hooked into a mesmerizing journey that promises to show the reader how to follow, not Mr. Nice Guy, but the 'Sensei of Shrewd.'"

Leonard Sweet, best-selling author, professor
at Drew University and George Fox University,
and chief contributor to Sermons.com

"Most of my life, I've felt guilty about dealing shrewdly with the world—particularly in the ultra-complex Middle East, where I serve. This book has not only given me permission to be shrewd but has provided the biblical framework for it. I encourage anyone who is following Jesus into this wild-ride big adventure in the real world to give this book a serious read."

Carl Medearis, author of *Speaking of Jesus*
and *Muslims, Christians, and Jesus*

"Rick Lawrence has done it again—he has unpacked a piece of Scripture in such a way that all who read this will forever change their paradigm of our roles as witnesses of Christ's love for us. *Shrewd* rattled my psyche and challenged me to embrace God in a new and demanding way. I wanted to cling to my concept of Jesus as a passive lamb, but now realize that the Jesus of the dark corners, who fights for my soul on a daily basis, is as shrewd as a snake but as innocent as a dove."

Donna S. Sheperis, PhD, counselor, professor,
clinical supervisor, and cochair of the American
Counseling Association Ethics Committee

"Rick has an astonishing way of taking the truth of Christ's teachings and translating them simply into the practice of daily living. He has taken a verse on which I have always stood and given it life and application to even my routine activities."

Teresa Weesner, director of development
for Providence Network

"It has been some time since a book has changed how I think in everyday ministry situations. *Shrewd* has done just that. Rick Lawrence redefines the leadership task in the balance of Jesus's imperative to be shrewd and innocent. *Shrewd* gets better with each turn of the page—a rare feat—and it will be on the reading list for my leadership classes."

Terry Linhart, PhD, chair of the Department of
Religion and Philosophy at Bethel College—Indiana

"*Shrewd* is part handbook for those wishing to minister to others and part exposé of the character of Jesus Christ. The book serves as a guide for engaging people to make an impact—ultimately on their eternity. Once again, Rick Lawrence has taken a verse of Scripture that many Christians have read with perhaps a vague understanding of its meaning and deconstructs the reader's individual schemata, resulting in a deeper, richer, more robust knowledge of who Jesus is and what He expects of us."

Robyn Trippany Simmons, PhD, professor
of counseling at Walden University

"*Shrewd* did a number on me—the idea got my attention as a ministry leadership value that I should have been thinking and talking about. Rick writes in a way that simultaneously messes with me and offers a hopeful vision for change. Before long I was doing revisionist rethinking about how I've operated as 'accidentally shrewd' in some situations, and resolved to be more intentional if I want to lead like Jesus, our perfectly shrewd Lord and King."

Dave Rahn, PhD, senior vice president and
chief ministry officer for Youth for Christ USA

"The tango I was dancing with the Holy Spirit was stiff, uncertain, and hesitant. I let others define my actions with their definitions and interpretations of how I should follow my dance partner. I now have permission to close my eyes, breathe Him in, and follow His bold, strong, and shrewd ways. My intimate dance with Jesus from here forward will be one of passionate trust. This is another of Rick Lawrence's books that I have decimated with dog-ears and highlights."

Michelle Pendergrass, author, publisher of
The Midnight Diner and *Relief Journal*, former president
of ccPublishing, mixed-media artist, and creator of
VisualPrayer.com and MichellePendergrass.com

"Disappointed with being pushed around and minimized in your spiritual life? Had enough of the mediocre? Tired of being on the losing side of a faith that often feels simplistic and ridiculous? You need to get *Shrewd*! Understanding and living into this rarely taught and profoundly transformative imperative can change everything in how you live a life of faith. Pick it up only if you want your bell rung. I read it and my ears are still ringing."

Dan Webster, founder of
Authentic Leadership, Inc.

Shrewd

Daring to Live the Startling Command of Jesus

RICK LAWRENCE

David C Cook®
transforming lives together

SHREWD
Published by David C Cook
4050 Lee Vance View
Colorado Springs, CO 80918 U.S.A.

David C Cook Distribution Canada
55 Woodslee Avenue, Paris, Ontario, Canada N3L 3E5

David C Cook U.K., Kingsway Communications
Eastbourne, East Sussex BN23 6NT, England

The graphic circle C logo is a registered trademark of David C Cook.

The website addresses recommended throughout this book are offered as a
resource to you. These websites are not intended in any way to be or imply an
endorsement on the part of David C Cook, nor do we vouch for their content.

Some names have been changed throughout to protect privacy.

All Scripture quotations, unless otherwise noted, are taken from the New American
Standard Bible®, Copyright © 1960, 1995 by The Lockman Foundation. Used
by permission. (www.Lockman.org.) Scripture quotations marked NIV are taken
from the Holy Bible, New International Version®, NIV®. Copyright © 1973,
1984 by Biblica, Inc™. Used by permission of Zondervan. All rights reserved
worldwide. www.zondervan.com; ESV are taken from The Holy Bible, English
Standard Version® (ESV®), copyright © 2001 by Crossway, a publishing ministry
of Good News Publishers. Used by permission. All rights reserved; MSG are taken
from *THE MESSAGE.* Copyright © by Eugene H. Peterson 1993, 2002. Used by
permission of NavPress Publishing Group; NLT are taken from the *Holy Bible,* New
Living Translation, copyright © 1996, 2007 by Tyndale House Foundation. Used by
permission of Tyndale House Publishers, Inc., Carol Stream, Illinois 60188. All rights
reserved; KJV are taken from the King James Version of the Bible. (Public Domain.)
The author has added italics to quotations for emphasis.

LCCN 2012935343
ISBN 978-1-4347-0073-5
eISBN 978-0-7814-0875-2

Published in association with the literary agency of WordServe Literary
Group, Ltd., 10152 S. Knoll Circle, Highlands Ranch, CO 80130.

The Team: Terry Behimer, John Blase, Amy Konyndyk,
Nick Lee, Caitlyn Carlson, Karen Athen
Cover Design: Brand Innovation Group

Printed in the United States of America
First Edition 2012

1 2 3 4 5 6 7 8 9 10

052912

To Beverly Rose, my beautiful crowbar.
And to Lucy Rose and Emma Grace, my treasured crowbar-ettes.

Acknowledgments

Thank you, Beverly Rose, for running the marathon with me—sometimes chasing me with a cattle prod, often surprising me with your grace, and even more often offering your blunt and passionate belief in me and in this work. You, my dear, have "levered" me into the man I am, by the grace and shrewdness of God.

Thank you, Lucy Rose and Emma Grace, for giving grace to an often-tired and sometimes distracted dad—I love our Saturday "R&B Jukebox" game nights, our weekend film fests, our personal pool parties, and our bedtime tell-alls. You are treasures.

Thank you, Tom Melton, for once again helping me find my way through the choking maze that obscures truth, and for introducing me to the traveling circus that is your reading list.

Thank you, Bob-Stud Krulish, for offering yourself, your friendship, and the stories of your life to me.

Thank you, Andy Brazelton, for encouraging and celebrating who I am with such ridiculous abandon. Actually, you do everything in your life with ridiculous abandon.

Thank you, Rick and Mary Jo Krump, for going so far above and beyond to fuel your advocacy of my writing life.

Thank you to those who read this manuscript in advance and offered both your encouragement and your critique: Beverly Rose, Mary Jo Krump, Bob Krulish, Jill Melton, Tom Melton, and Joe Marinich.

Thank you to all those who so generously gave me the space and real estate to write this labor of love: the monks of St. Benedict's Monastery, Gary and Deb Oberg, Rick and Mary Jo Krump, and the Mount St. Francis Retreat Center.

And since music is not just the backdrop to my creative life, but a fuel for it—a big thank-you to the artists who've been my accidental muses as I wrote this book: Steve Earle, Counting Crows, Sam Cooke, Gungor, Dispatch, Frank Sinatra, Ella Fitzgerald, Bruce Cockburn, Lucinda Williams, Rosie Thomas, Amos Lee, Andrew Osenga, The Normals, Andrew Peterson, Bob Dylan, Chicago, David Suomi & the Minor Prophets, Robert Randolph & the Family Band, Gillian Welch, Iron & Wine, The Low Anthem, Marc Cohn, Mavis Staples, Mindy Smith, Patty Griffin, Eddie Vedder, the Rolling Stones, Tonio K., U2, Van Morrison, Wilco, David Rawlings, the innocence mission, Jakob Dylan, John Coltrane, Johnny Hartman, Miles Davis, Mumford & Sons, Patty Larkin, The Raconteurs, Rich Mullins, Ray LaMontagne, Paul Simon, Stan Getz, The Secret Sisters, Wanda Jackson, and the Ramsey Lewis Trio.

And, finally, thank you, Greg Johnson at WordServe Literary, for your wise and surgical counsel. Thank you, Terry Behimer and Don Pape of David C Cook, for your continual advocacy of me. Thank you, Caitlyn Carlson, for catching the uncatchable. And, especially, thank you, John Blase, for dancing the tango so well with me—that sounds slightly more awkward than my intended meaning, but there you have it.

Contents

Introduction

In a tipping-point scene in the film *The Young Victoria*, the teen-aged Queen Victoria is playing chess with her future husband, the German-born Prince Albert. She knows Albert has been chosen by others to be her husband, and she's therefore both suspicious and intrigued by him. Already she is feeling the heat of political intrigue around her, and evil advisers are pressuring her to give up her right to succeed as Britain's queen and appoint a permanent caretaker (of their choosing) to the throne instead. As Albert and Victoria study the chessboard, they are also studying each other:

> **Victoria:** Do you ever feel like a chess piece, yourself? In a game being played against your will?
>
> **Albert:** Do you?
>
> **Victoria:** Constantly. I see them leaning in and moving me round the board.
>
> **Albert:** The Duchess and Sir John?
>
> **Victoria:** Not just them. Uncle Leopold. The King. I'm sure half the politicians are ready to seize hold of my skirts and drag me from square to square.
>
> **Albert:** Then you had better master the rules of the game until you play it better than they can.[1]

From this moment, Albert has Victoria hooked, because he recognizes what she most needs—an education in shrewdness. Victoria and Albert marry and become one of the great love stories in history, ruling the British Empire during its nineteenth-century glory days and deftly charting their own course through a quagmire of power-hungry despots and conniving members of their entourage.

At the center of their "glorious" rule is a centered commitment to act shrewdly—but as innocents. The "produce" of their great love is not just their nine children, but also revolutions in education, art, the sciences, social institutions that served the poor, and the anti-slavery movement. Together, they learn how to play the game of shrewd "better than their enemies."[2]

Like Victoria and Albert, people who understand and embrace Jesus's marching orders—"Be shrewd as serpents and innocent as doves" (Matt. 10:16)—are not afraid to pursue the leverage of shrewd in their everyday adventures, bringing life and light and freedom to those around them. Sometimes, they change the world. More often, they move through life, exercising redemptive leverage in one single life after another....

The Lurking Specter of Epic Consequence

Jesus describes the Holy Spirit as a "wind" that "blows where it wishes and you hear the sound of it, but do not know where it comes from and where it is going" (John 3:8). My middle schooler, Lucy, I've discovered, must be the Holy Spirit's twin ... or some other near relation. Because, in exactly the same way, a thirteen-year-old girl "talks where she wishes and I hear the sound of it, but do not know where it comes from and where it is going." It's happening again tonight as she stands next to our kitchen counter, doing her best to avoid going to bed at a decent hour. "Dad, I don't understand why Cammie won't come to church with me! Every time I ask her she has some excuse—she told me that church is dull and boring, and that's so wrong! If she would just come, even once, she'd see that church isn't what she thinks it is! But she just won't do it! It's so frustrating!"

That's five exclamation marks in a row, if you're counting....

So I toss an innocent little question at Lucy—it's a worm camouflaging a hook: "Hmmm. So, what do you think is at stake here for Cammie?"

"I don't understand what you mean."

"I mean, I think you're frustrated by her responses and excuses because you don't really understand what's going on in Cammie—you haven't yet considered the possible reasons why the cost of accepting your invitation is so high for her. All of your direct approaches to overcome Cammie's reluctance have not worked. So, what's at stake for her?"

"Ummm ... well, she doesn't want to be bored, I guess."

"But you've told her that church isn't boring, and you've asked her to just try it out once with you. What if she thought, 'If I say yes to her once, that'll mean I have to say no a million times after that, because I don't want to go to church'?"

"But why is she so against it?"

"Well, let's try to understand what might be going on inside her. Maybe it has little to do with her true opinion of church. If she says yes to going to church with you, it might mean she has to choose for or against a big change in her life, and maybe she's just not ready for a big change. Her parents are divorced, her dad doesn't seem to care about her very much, and she and her mom have vowed that they're going to make it on their own. Maybe going to church seems like an admission of weakness."

"I guess that's possible."

"Or what if she just wants to sleep in on Sunday mornings, and if she says yes, that will mean she'll have to constantly find an alternate excuse to explain why she wants to continue to sleep in on Sundays? But she's embarrassed to admit that, so she'll have to work pretty hard to come up with a bunch of non-embarrassing excuses."

"I guess that's really, really possible."

"So, understanding these possibilities, and that your approach so far has utterly failed"—(a wry smile from Lucy)—"how can you approach this differently? What could you do that might exert enough leverage to move her toward accepting your invitation?"

"Well, what if I asked her to come to church with me, and *then* invited her to come home afterward to hang out? I think she would like that."

"That's worth trying. And what about this: what if you invited her to come to a fun outing with your youth group—something not at the church, and obviously a one-time event? Like that bowling thing you're going to do, for example. If there's no ongoing commitment implied, maybe she'll take your bait."

And just as quickly as it blew in, the hurricane moves offshore. Lucy gives me a half smile and wanders away to her bedroom as the gears in her head grind away. And tomorrow, when Cammie least expects it, I think she's going to get leveraged by the shrewdest middle schooler in our zip code. Her determination to avoid church at all costs is about to come under benevolent assault—the same kind of benevolent assault that is at the core of God's redemptive pursuit of His wayward children. Lucy and I weren't just bantering over our kitchen counter; we were *plotting*. And an everyday conversation about friction and frustration in a friendship morphed into a strategic conversation that could change history—*Cammie's history.*

For Cammie, the question of whether Lucy can figure out how to get past her defenses and convince her to give church a taste may actually mark the difference between life and death. Remember what Robert Frost wrote: "Two roads diverged in a wood, and I— / I took the one less traveled by, / and that has made all the difference."[3] It's not hard to see the "two roads" in front of Cammie and how she's already headed down the road "most traveled." Our choice of roads does "make all the difference"—Jesus delivers a blunt truth when He says there are "many" who walk through the "wide" gate and travel the "broad" way that "leads to destruction" (Matt. 7:13). It's that faint sense of *epic consequence* that is fueling Lucy's passion to nudge Cammie onto the narrow way that leads to life.

And the specter of *epic consequence* is all around us—sometimes hiding behind the kitchen counter where a thirteen-year-old girl is venting about her thwarted attempts to help a friend find the "living water" she doesn't know she needs, and sometimes jabbing a finger at us from the front-page headlines on every newspaper in the world....

A Hurricane in Disguise

In late February 2011 two brutal dictators—both of them savvy and determined despots who'd managed to keep their stranglehold on power for more than two decades—quickly discovered that their political skills were no match for a decentralized opposition movement led by no-name students and hardscrabble revolutionaries with no political experience and little organizational structure. In both Tunisia and Egypt, the immovable met the unrelenting—and in the space of a few weeks, the unsinkable presidents Zine al-Abidine Ben Ali and Hosni Mubarak were taking on water faster than the Titanic.

The whole world was caught off guard by the shocking speed of democratic revolution in the Middle East. In the middle of this earthquake, a stunned reporter with the *Chicago Tribune* had trouble chewing and then ingesting the unbelievable truth:

> A couple of weeks ago, the human rights group Freedom House rated the Middle East, with its host of despotic regimes, the most repressed region of the planet. But that was a couple of weeks ago. At the moment, opposition to dictators is spreading fast and putting authoritarian governments in peril.... The "Jasmine Revolution" [in Tunisia] marks the first time that a popular movement had toppled the government of an Arab country. The Tunisian example was noted by its neighbors, and soon, throngs of Egyptians were taking to the streets demanding an end to the reign of President Hosni Mubarak, who has had a lock on power since 1981.[4]

It's easy to miss a colossal statement buried in the *Trib*'s summation: "*the first time* ... a popular movement had toppled the government of an Arab country ..."

Why this time and not another? Why these countries and not others? Why these despots and not others? Of course, the answers to these questions are, at least in part, metaphysical—not everything is a cause-and-effect strategy, and not everything is a linear progression toward an expected outcome. But there is an eighty-three-year-old retired American professor of political science living in Boston—a shuffling and fragile academic who walks with a cane and looks nothing like a revolutionary—who knows the answers to these questions, because he helped bring these autocratic regimes down. Protestors in Tunisia and Egypt—and in a half dozen other countries—have used Dr. Gene Sharp's little masterwork *From Dictatorship to Democracy* as a blueprint for nonviolent revolution, making the professor's cluttered hobbit-hole of an office ground-zero for an unprecedented worldwide surge toward democratic reform. Rebel groups on every continent outside of Antarctica have translated, reprinted, and downloaded Sharp's "198 nonviolent weapons" over and over, using them as the rocket fuel for revolution.[5]

In the days after the fall of Mubarak, *Morning Edition* host Steve Inskeep tracked down Sharp for an interview—Inskeep was looking for the "secret sauce" in the aging man's recipe for regime change. What Inskeep discovered at the core of Sharp's approach was a weapons-grade tactic—a way of thinking and acting called *shrewd*—that Jesus long ago urged His followers to use in their own nonviolent uprising against the powers and spiritual forces of wickedness of this world. Shrewd people (and Jesus is the Exemplar) first study how things work[6] and then leverage that knowledge to tip the balance in a favored direction. Both Ben Ali and Mubarak rammed their dictatorships right into that lurking iceberg named *shrewd*—but you likely never heard the word on CNN or saw it in your local newspaper because, just like an iceberg, you see only its tip breaking the surface. To get a better feel for what *shrewd* looks like, play "Where's Waldo?" with this short interchange between Inskeep and Dr. Sharp—you'll find it hiding in plain sight:

Inskeep: What is necessary in order to have a realistic plan for a nonviolent protest against a dictatorship?

Dr. Sharp: First of all, if you're living under a dictator, you really have to know that particular system extremely well, including its weaknesses, because dictators are never as powerful as they tell you they are. Secondly, you need to understand nonviolent struggle extremely well. And finally, you need to be able to think strategically.

Inskeep: Think strategically—meaning, don't just don't create chaos, create a better situation.

Dr. Sharp: You need to determine: what are you going to do first? Do you identify weaknesses in the regime that are dependent on certain sources of power? How can you cut those sources of power off in order to weaken the dictatorship's power?

Inskeep: Why is nonviolent resistance preferable to violent resistance?

Dr. Sharp: Because it's wise. Why should you choose to fight with your enemy's best weapons?

That doesn't make sense at all. Nonviolent struggle is a kind of people-power. You have a much greater chance of succeeding by you choosing the means that they're not equipped to deal with effectively.[7]

The Right Force at the Right Time in the Right Place

Protesters in both Tunisia and Egypt used shrewd leverage, like a crowbar, to pry two stubborn hubcaps away from their positions of power. And while "crowbar" accurately captures the way shrewdness applies leverage, it doesn't convey its artistic beauty. Dr. Sharp may be a political scientist, but he is more truly an artist working in the medium of nonviolent resistance, advocating the use of leverage to bring freedom to captives. And if "using leverage to bring freedom to captives" sounds familiar, it's because that's a fair rendering of Jesus's job description (Luke 4:18). He's the original Artist—His canvas is the people He created and loves, His vision is to set His people free from the penalty and influence of sin, and His paintbrush is dipped in shrewd. What happened on the cross and in the empty tomb was, truly, the expert application of leverage on behalf of our freedom. What He has done—and is doing in your life right now, at the moment you are reading these words—is fueled not only by His passionate love for you but by His relentlessly shrewd pursuit of you. He is using shrewd crowbar leverage *right now* to pry you from your captivity, whatever it is, and free you to worship Him more wholeheartedly.

And we know that God causes all things to work
together for good to those who love God, to
those who are called according to His purpose.
(Rom. 8:28)

Though it seems strange to the taste, "caus[ing] all things to
work together for good" is a fair definition of shrewdness that is
tempered by what Jesus called "innocence." The reason Jesus urged
His disciples, in Matthew 10, to "be shrewd as serpents and innocent as doves" (v. 16) is, simply, because our fundamental charge is
to "be perfect, as your heavenly Father is perfect" (Matt. 5:48) and
to "grow up in all aspects into Him who is the head, even Christ"
(Eph. 4:15). And as we become more perfected in Christ—a slow
metamorphosis born out of our deepening attachment to Him—we
will necessarily become more simultaneously shrewd and innocent,
because that is what He is at His core. Dr. Sharp well understands
this fundamental aspect of Jesus, though he does not recognize
Jesus as the primary model for it and never mentions Him in his
work. The art of shrewd, described by Dr. Sharp in his interview
with Steve Inskeep, most closely resembles the improvisational
interplay of a jazz quartet:

- First, *study how things work* until you have a thor-
  ough understanding of the patterns, rhythms,
  strengths, and weaknesses of the person or regime or
  organization or issue you're targeting. (*"If you're living
  under a dictator, you really have to know that particular
  system extremely well."*)

- **Second, based on your understanding of how things work, *choose a point of leverage* to go after.** *("You need to determine: what are you going to do first?")*

- **Third, *apply some leverage* and see what happens.** *("How can you cut those sources of power off in order to weaken the dictatorship's power?")*

- **Fourth, *repeat the cycle* until you've learned how to apply just the right leverage in just the right place and at the right time to move the situation in your favor.** *("You have a much greater chance of succeeding by you choosing the means that they're not equipped to deal with effectively.")*

Dr. Sharp is describing the rhythm of *shrewd* played out on a grand scale—it's a behavioral strategy specifically crafted for sheep to use in the company of wolves, a necessary but nearly neglected way of thinking for an outnumbered and outgunned people who live in enemy territory. Our reality, whether or not we acknowledge it, is that we must contend every day with "the world forces of this darkness" (Eph. 6:12). And our strategic frontal assaults against these forces have minimal long-term impact, just as a military force built for nation-state conflicts has long since been exposed as ineffective in an age of surgical terrorism. Terrorists—both seen and unseen—use tactics that exert leverage on their enemies, making it possible for a relative handful of shrewd fighters to bring armies and nations to their knees. This is why the outnumbered and outgunned terrorist named Lucifer continues to "steal, kill, and destroy"—he's not at all shy about attacking his enemies (the children of God), using shrewd leverage. And just as Western military leaders have learned to adjust their frontal-assault thinking in order to combat tiny bands of shrewd terrorists, so the children of God must heed Jesus's call to shrewdness and modify their battle strategy.

Simply, shrewdness is the expert application of leverage—a little thing that levers a big thing. In his book *The Way Things Work*, renowned architect David Macaulay describes the essence of how shrewd leverage *moves things*:

> Mechanical machines all deal with forces. In one
> way they are just like people when it comes to getting them on the move: it always takes some effort.
> Movement does not simply occur of its own accord,
> even when you drop something. It needs a driving
> force—the push of a motor, the pull of muscles or
> gravity, for example. In a machine, this driving force
> must then be conveyed to the right place in the right
> amount.[8]

Applying the right amount of force in the right place at the right time is exactly how shrewd works. In Romans 5 the apostle Paul describes how shrewdness—force/place/time—is at work in the heart of God: "For while we were still helpless, *at the right time* Christ died for the ungodly" (v. 6). In Christ we have the right force (the Son of God) coming to the right place (the land of the Jews, God's "chosen" people) at the right time (during the height of the Greco-Roman world). And once He'd infiltrated behind enemy lines, Jesus was always studying how things worked, then applying the right force in the right place at the right time to advance the kingdom of God on earth.

Later we'll study much of what Jesus said and did through the lens of shrewd, but here's a random example of His *right force/right place/right time* rhythm: in John 7 Jesus's disbelieving brothers urge Him to travel with them to the Feast of Booths in Judea, cynically prodding Him to declare Himself in public so that His "disciples also may see [His] works which [He is] doing" (v. 3). But Jesus understands, just as His scheming brothers do, that the Jews in Judea are "seeking to kill Him" (v. 1). So He responds: "My time is not yet here, but your time is always opportune" (v. 6). In effect, He's telling them: "I have the right amount of force, but this is not the right place or the right time to use it. However, if you'd like to get yourself killed, have at it." So the thwarted brothers leave without Him. A few verses later Jesus travels to the Feast anyway, "going up in secret." There He unveils Himself in the time and place and way that *He's chosen.*

The One Parable We've Never Heard in Church

Though shrewdness is embedded in Jesus's personality and high-lighted as a crucial way of thinking for sheep surrounded by wolves, we are (by Jesus's own assessment) very poor practitioners of it. This hard diagnosis is at the core of perhaps His least-known and most inscrutable teaching: the Parable of the Shrewd Manager. In the story He spotlights a no-good, conniving, lazy man whose only admirable characteristic, according to Jesus, is his ability to understand how things work, then apply the right force in the right place at the right time to move things in his favor.

The Parable of the Shrewd Manager
(Luke 16:1–8 NIV)

Jesus told his disciples: "There was a rich man whose manager was accused of wasting his possessions. So he called him in and asked him, 'What is this I hear about you? Give an account of your management, because you cannot be manager any longer.'

"The manager said to himself, 'What shall I do now? My master is taking away my job. I'm not strong enough to dig, and I'm ashamed to beg—I know what I'll do so that, when I lose my job here, people will welcome me into their houses.'

"So he called in each one of his master's debtors. He asked the first, 'How much do you owe my master?'

"'Eight hundred gallons of olive oil,' he replied.

"The manager told him, 'Take your bill, sit down quickly, and make it four hundred.'

"Then he asked the second, 'And how much do you owe?'

"'A thousand bushels of wheat,' he replied.

"He told him, 'Take your bill and make it eight hundred.'

"The master commended the dishonest manager because he had acted shrewdly. For the people of this world are more shrewd in dealing with their own kind than are the people of the light."

When I first explored this bizarre story with my own congregation, I titled my message "The One Parable You've Never Heard in Church." Sure enough, when the service ended, lots of people stopped to tell me they'd not only never heard anything like this in church, they didn't even know the parable was in the Bible. As I was making my way out of the sanctuary to collect my kids from Sunday school, a man who is a successful personal injury lawyer was standing in the shadows—he reached out to shake my hand. With tears welling in his eyes he leaned over and whispered in my ear: "I'm the shrewdest person I know. And today, for the first time, I felt like who I *really* am is okay to bring into church." He moved back into the shadows with a slight and grateful smile on his face.

Did Jesus *really* tell a story about a conniving jerk, then urge His followers to think and behave more like, well … *this guy*? Well, yes. And even more to the point, Jesus is telling us we're sorely deficient in something the "people of the world" have in spades. And He's telling us, for some reason, that our deficiency is not good for the kingdom of God.

Jesus's Parable of the Shrewd Manager startles and offends us, like a belching debutante at a tea party. We expect our Christianity—and our Messiah, for that matter—to conform to the sort of good guys/bad guys template that Christian culture has worked so hard to ingrain in us. We have, as A. W. Tozer observes, taken the Jesus of the Bible and bent Him into "a very well-behaved God."[9] So, when He calls the Pharisees "whitewashed tombs" (Matt. 23:27) and "vipers" (v. 33) and "son[s] of hell" (v. 15), we tell ourselves He's not really cursing them, because it's an uneasy fit with our pristine ideas about Him. And when He refuses to offer healing to the daughter of the Canaanite woman (15:22–26), calling her a "dog" in the process, we tell ourselves that "dog" must have been a backhanded compliment way back then, because Jesus would never purposefully offend anyone. And when He warns His disciples (18:6) that any adult who causes "one of these little ones … to stumble" will experience a fate worse than forced drowning, it doesn't truly register that "better for him to have a heavy millstone hung around his neck" is a decidedly un-nice thing to say.

The manager in Jesus's story is an unsavory person in every way, and it makes no sense that our gracious, well-behaved, soft-spoken, clean-cut Savior is telling us to pattern our lives after him. "Well, that's Jesus for you," we tell ourselves. "He doesn't have to explain Himself, because He's God." And this is just another subtle way we explain away the greatness of God, another way we disrespect Him, another missed opportunity to worship a Father and a Son and a Spirit who are all *good* beyond our hopes. The grizzled Old Testament prophet Isaiah did his best to warn people that the promised Messiah would shatter their expectations: "He will be a stone that causes men to stumble and a rock that makes them fall" (Isa. 8:14 NIV). Jesus has always been and always will be misunderstood. We continuously edit Him to fit our expectations and quell our fears, and by doing so we necessarily stop believing in Him because the *Him* we are believing in—the partial and palatable Jesus—does not exist. But Paul, author of most of the New Testament, and Peter, the first leader of the church, both use Isaiah's *stumbling stone* words to describe the Jesus they knew so intimately. For example, Paul in Romans 9:33 says, "Behold, I lay in Zion a stone of stumbling and a rock of offense, and he who believes in Him will not be disappointed," and Peter in 1 Peter 2:7–8 writes, "The Stone which the builders rejected, this became the very corner stone … a stone of stumbling and a rock of offense." It's ironic that Paul, just after warning us that Jesus will make us stumble, tells us that if we will only believe in Him we "will not be disappointed." The shattering we experience when we draw near to Jesus will lead to something deeper and better than we know how to ask Him for.

Despite Paul's certainty about our reaction to the "Rock of Offense," it's clear that if we studied the Jesus described in the Bible, we'd discover He is simultaneously the incarnation of God and the most confounding and *difficult* person who has ever lived. We can't force His Parable of the Shrewd Manager down our throats without choking. But if we are to trust Paul's "[you] will not be disappointed," then we will have to move past our initial repulsion for the "hero" in Jesus's parable and plunge, like a blind explorer, into the great unknown of His goodness.

The Sheep and the Wolves

It's important to revisit what was motivating Jesus to tell this story at this exact time and place: a "great multitude" has gathered around

Him because they've never heard teaching like His and have never seen miracles like His. Even "the tax gatherers and the sinners" (Luke 15:1) can't help themselves; they are like gawkers at a traffic accident who can't stop staring at the spectacle that is Jesus. And, of course, any young rabbi who draws a *rabble* following is going to rivet the attention of the self-righteous scribes and Pharisees, who gossip and carp about Jesus slumming with these people.

With the sheep and the wolves thus congregated, Jesus selects His scalpel. And, like a surgeon surrounded by med students, He makes a few quick incisions in the polished skin of the Pharisees, slicing them with a quick succession of stories that expose the cancer that has invaded their hearts. At first, the stories are about rescue—finding the lost sheep, discovering the lost coin, and welcoming home the lost son. He's revealing the heart of God, which is driven by a passion for redemption. Then, He follows with a stroke that cuts more deeply than the others: a story-stab about a rich man's admiration for his blundering, lazy, cowardly, and conniving manager. Here, encircled by the menacing wolf pack—Jesus offers His helpless sheep a secret weapon.

The Parable of the Shrewd Manager describes the kingdom of God's "rules of engagement" for those who would follow Him—a people Jesus compares to an animal that has no natural defenses against the predators that hunt it. When He tells His disciples, on the eve of their first missionary journey without Him along for the ride, *"Be as shrewd as snakes and as innocent as doves"* (NIV), this is not a rhetorical flourish. Jesus is choosing His words carefully, because He knows His closest friends are about to plunge into a meat grinder. He's trying to describe their reality and our reality—that, in fact, the people of God are defenseless, dependent, and slow-on-the-uptake prey who are surrounded by conniving predators. Because that is true ("Therefore"), we must "live and breathe and move" in these two seemingly dichotomous character traits:

1. Shrewdness—understanding how things work, then leveraging that knowledge to apply the right force in the right place at the right time.
2. Innocence—freedom from guilt of any kind.

Shrewd as serpents and innocent as doves. When Jesus uses the word *snake* as a descriptor for shrewd, He's choosing the same word that, elsewhere in Scripture, describes Satan—in Hebrew it's *nachash*, the identical word Moses uses in Genesis 3:1 to describe God's Enemy. And when He uses the word *dove* as a descriptor for innocence, He chooses the same word that, elsewhere in Scripture, describes the Holy Spirit. Jesus is saying, bluntly, that His disciples must be as shrewd as Satan is but not evil as Satan is. He's essentially telling us that we must beat Satan (and those in his service) at his own game by practicing a greater level of shrewdness than he does, but with none of his cruel intent or evil motivation. And something about that still doesn't sound right. Satan is evil, right? Why would we do *anything* the way he does it? The Parable of the Shrewd Manager, and Jesus's specific instructions to His disciples when they head off without Him for the first time, are two big potholes we must swerve to avoid when we're reading the Bible. When we do swerve around His shrewd imperative, *we miss Jesus*. And because Jesus is "the exact representation of His nature" (Heb. 1:3), we also miss the heart of God the Father. Even more, we ignore the most important tool we've been given as people called to "make disciples of all the nations" (Matt. 28:19).

Be the Croc

If you have shrewd people in your life, you know they operate like can openers, peeling back your carefully maintained veneer to poke at your tender spots—it's not really "safe" (in the conventional sense) to be vulnerable around people who are shrewd. That's because shrewd people leverage every situation in their preferred direction— for good or for evil. My friend Aik Hong Tan buys struggling luxury hotels, renovates them, then reopens them as thriving businesses. I ask him to give me his definition of shrewd, and he says: "Shrewd is a way of dealing with people—it means understanding their motives and understanding my own motives, and then discovering how I can reconcile the two." I ask, "What do you mean by 'reconciling the two'?" And he explains, a little sheepishly: "It's a way of doing things that brings about results—the results *I want*.... Shrewd is a neutral word. It's just a means to an end. But most [Christians] think it smells rotten. I don't."[10] When I ask my old friend John, a lawyer and business leader in a Christian family-owned real-estate business, to ask his coworkers if they see shrewdness as a positive or negative thing, he tells me their response is unanimously positive. "So why," I ask, "is shrewd seen as such an ugly word in the church?" His answer is blunt and true: "Rick, the church trains people to be nice."[11]

Remember the old fable of the crocodile who convinced the frog that he could safely ferry him across a river on his tail, then progressively convinced the frog he'd have a better view of the river from his nose, then promptly turned the frog into an appetizer?[12] That's a perfect illustration of a person who uses shrewdness to "get the results he wants." These people are dangerous—for good or for evil. And nice people are nothing like them—they are stout, trusting, conscientious, diligent, forgiving, trustworthy, perseverant, pleasant, and accommodating (yeah, just like that frog). They go out of their way to make you feel comfortable at your small-group meeting—a real contrast to the shrewd person who makes you feel … nervous. Jesus makes people nervous too—nervous because the kingdom of God is in their face. Nervous because He's always saying and doing leveraging things that are crafted to bring the results He wants. Stab your finger anywhere in one of the Gospels, and you'll find an example of Jesus talking and acting shrewdly. Just now I flipped open the Bible that sits next to my computer and landed in Matthew 17, where a man is asking Jesus to cast out a demon from his lunatic son because the disciples had failed at the task. Jesus quickly rebukes them, rebukes the demon, then advises: "This kind does not go out except by prayer and fasting" (v. 21). Jesus studies how things work ("this kind"), then leverages what He learns to apply the right force ("prayer and fasting") at the right time and in the right place.

Metaphorically, Jesus implores, "Be the crocodile, not the frog." You won't find that slogan on a Precious Moments poster or, real-istically, in any sermon in any church in America. In His story of the shrewd manager and in His marching orders for His disciples, Jesus tells us that shrewdness is a daily necessity. It's not listed as a fruit of the spirit or a beatitude or a prerequisite for a Proverbs 31 woman, but, nevertheless, it's *definitely* the reason we're sitting here redeemed and restored into relationship with God. It's *most certainly* the engine behind every great movement of God and every advance of His kingdom. And, closer to our everyday consciousness, it's also the reason why:

- some marriages are marked by deeper intimacy and joy;
- some parents mold more mature, enjoyable, and savvy children;
- some businesses continue to grow during hard times;
- some physicians are consistently better at getting their patients well;
- some people leave behind them a wake of healing and restoration;
- some households in your neighborhood live better with less;
- some church leaders turn "we've always done it this way" on its ear;
- some missionaries are rescuing women caught up in human trafficking;
- some commanders turn a battlefield quagmire into victory; and, less expected,
- some people are closer, and more continually close, to Jesus in spirit and practice.

Because we've never thought of Jesus as the shrewdest man who ever lived, or spent much time paying attention to what the Bible says about shrewdness, it's simply off our radar as integral to our life with

Christ. And that's exactly why Jesus told the Parable of the Shrewd Manager—He knew the people of God were *woefully unshrewd* at engaging others (and at engaging "principalities" and "powers" and "rulers of the darkness of this world" and "spiritual wickedness in high places"—Eph. 6:12 KJV).

How shrewd are you? For most of us, that's the first time we've ever considered the question. It's not the sort of conversation starter that goes down well at the church picnic. We don't regale our friends with our great feats of shrewdness at work, at home, and in our "Living Like Jesus" class at church. So what will be our response to Jesus's charge to move more shrewdly, anchored by the heart of an innocent?

Chapter 1

Shrewd as Serpents, Innocent as Doves

All machines that use mechanical parts are built with the same
single aim: to ensure that exactly the right amount of force produces
just the right amount of movement precisely where it is needed.
—David Macaulay, in his introduction to *The Way Things Work*

He who works with his hands and his head and his heart is an artist.
—St. Francis of Assisi

If there is one terrible disease in the Church of Christ, it is that we
do not see God as great as He is. We're too familiar with God.
—A. W. Tozer, "Worship: The Missing Jewel"

Not long ago I was at a large fund-raiser dinner for a ministry my
family has supported for years. I brought my video camera along to

record interviews, asking a roomful of longtime Christians to give me their definition of *shrewd*. These are the exact words and phrases they used in their definitions:

- Conniving
- Sneaky
- Sly
- Underground
- Clever with a touch of calculation
- Mean
- Coarse, rude, and unbecoming
- Crafty and good at getting what they want
- Good at getting money and not very happy—not very fun

And perhaps my favorite response, because it's so snarky...

- A German warship from the 1800s[1]

Ah, the Good Ship Shrewd—it's almost impossible for us to keep from infecting the word with negativity. We'd never praise a friend, for example, by saying: "I really admire you—you're the most conniving person I know!" And you won't find a single greeting card that reads: "Thanks for the way you've been cunning in my life." It's hard to separate *shrewd* from its negative connotations, but in truth, it's a neutral force that can be used for good or for evil. And even though Dr. Sharp describes *shrewd* at work in an epic moment in history, its more natural and much broader application is in our everyday encounters, opportunities, and challenges. All of us intrinsically understand the basics of leverage in our relationships—when I give my kids a consequence for disrespectful behavior, they often stop behaving disrespectfully—but most of us have done little to harness that leverage in service to the kingdom of God. We are shrewd accidentally, and often not innocently. That's why so many of our deepest hopes and dreams suffer shipwreck—we've paid little or no attention to the clear imperative Jesus delivered to His disciples: "Be shrewd as serpents but innocent as doves."

Shrewdness Hiding in Plain Sight

People all around us are studying how things work, all the time, then using leverage to gain a favored outcome. Pry the lid off any vocation, and you'll find shrewd people acting shrewdly. Not long ago a principal in a San Francisco school conducted an experiment. He told three of his teachers that, because they'd been recognized as three of the district's best instructors, they'd been assigned ninety high-IQ students with a charge to see how far they could take them academically. By year's end, these students had achieved about 25 percent more than their peers. The principal then came clean: he'd given the teachers "average" students chosen at random. Furthermore, he'd chosen the three teachers by drawing their names from a hat.[2] By studying how things work in his school—paying attention to what motivates both students and teachers—the principal produced an astonishing surge in academic progress, leveraging both kids and adults toward his goal of a higher-achieving school.

Even though we're mostly oblivious to it, acts of shrewdness are lurking behind every big moment in our history, no matter where we plant our finger on the time line. A random case in point: after landing on the moon in 1969, the astronauts of Apollo 11 were hurtling back toward earth when a potentially catastrophic failure threatened their safe return. A failed bearing in the turret of a powerful antenna at the NASA tracking station in Guam had knocked the antenna out of service—it was the last line of communication with Apollo 11 before splashdown. The whole world waited on the edge of its seat as the crisis deepened. Meanwhile, fourth-grader Greg Force sat at home with his mom and three brothers while his dad, Guam tracking-station director Charles Force, monitored communications with the spacecraft as it headed toward reentry. Charles knew there was no time to replace the bearing before the capsule entered earth's atmosphere, so he did some quick (and shrewd) thinking. If he could pack a little more grease around the failed bearing, the antenna might work long enough to get Apollo 11 safely home. But the access hole was just two-and-a-half inches in diameter, and nobody at the station had an arm small enough to reach the bearing. So Charles had someone race to his home and pick up Greg, whose skinny little arm reached through the tiny hole and packed grease around the failed bearing. It worked, and Apollo 11 splashed down safely. Mr. Force found a way to use the right force in the right place at the right time.[3]

These are standout examples of shrewdness in play, to be sure, but maybe the biggest surprise is how often the people who are closest to us—and even our own surprising selves—speak and act shrewdly. Aik Hong Tan says: "[Shrewd is] just like parenting kids—you can say 'It's my way or the highway,' but that's being a tyrant. Instead, you study to understand their leanings or tendencies—all kids are different. And when you understand their natural leanings you'll know how to apply the right style of teaching."[4] So we study how things work, come to grips with our "favored outcome," then apply the right force in the right place at the right time to move the situation in that direction. This is no rhetorical exercise, by the way—this kind of progressive thinking can make a huge difference in almost all our everyday relational challenges. A case in point: the thirty-minute conversation I had with my wife today.

To satisfy our daily craving for uninterrupted conversation (our two girls = constant chatter), Bev and I often take a walk around a two-mile loop in our neighborhood. On the menu of topics today is her strong response to a friend in another state who is acting self-absorbed, rigid, insecure, and arrogant. For the last five years or so, this friend has been unable to accept a very painful reality in her life. Because of that, this woman is often bemoaning her situation, frequently directing conversations back to the source of her pain. Bev has, so far, simply offered her patient support, encouragement, and honest feedback, but today I can tell she's reached a tipping point—she's gearing up to unload a piece of her mind on her friend. About halfway into our walk I start wondering what shrewdness would look like in this coming confrontation, so I ask: "Just for the sake of experiment, and given the insights you already have, would you be willing to consider how you could engage your friend more shrewdly on all of this?" She tells me she'd first need to express to me exactly what she wishes she could say to her friend directly.

When she's finished explaining her very understandable response, I ask: "You've explained your perspective very well, but what about my question?" She responds, very authentically I think: "That seems like work to me, and I don't know if I want to work that hard at this." And I'm nodding my head in agreement because I know just where she's coming from—no doubt, shrewd responses *do* take work. That's why so many of us, including me, aren't shrewd most of the time. But when a friendship is riding on that response, it seems worth the effort, and that's what I say to Bev. "Just for the sake of the experiment," I ask, "what's something in your life that feels a lot like the painful reality in your friend's life?" She quickly reels off two things that fit the description. Then I think for a moment and offer this: "If you can connect with her on a feeling level by understanding your own struggles to accept the 'pain elephant in your room,' then maybe you can win the right to say something about the way she's struggling." Maybe, I venture, as Bev thinks about her own responses to the painful realities of her life, she could simply extend that interior conversation to her friend. I say, "Maybe this would help you communicate that you are *for* her as a preamble to you saying a hard thing to her."

My wife is quiet, deep in thought, churning through what I'm saying, opening herself to the experiment. Then I ask: "How do you typically respond to someone you know is not *for* you?" She looks at me and says, "Not well." I hold my hands out in front of me like a stop sign and say, "Like this?" She nods and gets quiet again. She's doing the "hard work" of crafting a shrewder response to her friend—considering how to apply the right force in the right place at the right time to move her friend out of the prison of victimhood and into a place of freedom. Ten minutes later, after I'm back at my desk at home, Bev reminds me of why I love her so much.

She could have been frustrated with my feedback, but, instead, she comes into my office and thanks me for our conversation: "I really needed that—you not only challenged me to think through a shrewd way to bring this up to my friend, you also challenged me to be *for* her instead of against her." And this is what it means to wrestle with the best way to apply force in the right place at the right time. It *is* work, but only because we're so unpracticed at it. Thankfully, we can get through most of our everyday interactions using our relational default setting—openhearted and direct—as long as we're prepared to live and move and breathe shrewdly when it's warranted. And to do that we'll have to set aside our natural revulsion for shrewd's darker roots.

The Dark Art of Old Man Potter

To be labeled shrewd is an insult to most Christians—only scoundrels, ne'er-do-wells, and the pirates of Wall Street wear the description well. This is why we're not at all surprised, for example, when a wicked character in a film acts shrewdly—that's just what wicked characters do. A case in point ...

Among the many moments that sear like parables in the classic holiday film *It's a Wonderful Life*[5] is the scene where Old Man Potter tries to convince the young, self-sacrificing George Bailey to join him in his predatory business ventures. Potter is a craggy, bitter, small-town robber baron amassing a fortune by siphoning every bit of financial margin from the poor working-class fathers and mothers who are forced to deal with him. His great purpose in life is to dominate—to capture and control all sources of power and commerce in little old Bedford Falls, no matter what the cost. His food is the freedom of others, and he fills his belly with the fruits of his narcissism. Shrewdness is his weapon of choice, of course. So he first *studies how George works* to discover what motivates him, then surgically leverages his barely hidden resentments, heartbreaks, and longings for his own purposes. This is what the cycle of shrewd looks like from Potter's perspective:

1. George has a lifelong dream to do something really big in the world, but that dream has continually, repeatedly been subjugated to responsibility, duty, and service. So, shrewdly, Potter offers him a job that promises him a slightly twisted, and ultimately evil, version of his dreams.

2. George has always had a wanderlust, dreaming of world travel from the time he was a boy. But every opportunity has slipped through his fingers, repeatedly and sometimes at the last moment. So, shrewdly, Potter promises him a couple of trips to Europe every year if he will abandon his ideals and accept a position with his firm.

3. George's self-sacrificing leadership of his dead father's low-margin Building & Loan has condemned him to perpetual financial pressures at home. So, shrewdly, Potter offers him ten times his current salary, wiping out his greatest source of daily stress.

If you set aside your obvious disgust for Potter as a person, you must admit he's the smartest person in the film, right up until the end—he has shrewdly studied the pressure points of frustration and wounding in George's life, has discovered how they are motivating him, and then applies the right force in the right place at the right time. He's determined to destroy George and everything he represents, but Potter has been repeatedly thwarted when he's used a more direct approach. So he concocts a much shrewder plan—he comes at George sideways, from a place of surprising leverage that wobbles George's seemingly unshakeable integrity.

In a pivotal scene in the film, George lights up the expensive cigar Potter offers him, and the smoke from it curls around his head like a poisonous wreath. The leverage is working. George, for a moment hypnotized, is living in the alternate universe Potter has painted for him, and the one man in the film who can be counted on for his virtue is *this close* to giving it all away. It's only when George reaches across Potter's massive desk to shake his hand that the spell is broken—the touch of the evil man's hand awakens George to the poisonous vapors that fill the room, and he comes to his senses. As George's head clears, he responds with fury. The fury is directed more toward himself than it is toward Potter, because Potter has come *this close* to stealing his soul for "a mess of pottage," and George is incensed at himself for even considering it.

The story, as you know, ends in fairy-tale fashion—happily ever after. A rescuing angel named Clarence arrives to give George the gift of seeing what the world would be like if he'd never been born. The gaping truth of his never-born existence sets off a chain reaction of misery and darkness for his family and everyone in the small town of Bedford Falls. He recoils from the experience, and his desperation leads to a rebirth … rather literally. And so, through the generosity of all of those who've benefited from George's selfless love over the years, Potter is thwarted. Niceness wins in the end, and shrewdness is punished. There's only one problem with the rise and fall of shrewd Old Man Potter in this film.…

In real life, Potter would've squashed George like a fly.

People like Potter—cunning and committed and shrewdly evil—make appetizers out of nice, principled guys who are repelled and surprised by their enemy's "dirty work." George Bailey is a virtuous metronome, a sheep unaware that he's been tagged for slaughter (just as the apostle Paul described the followers of Jesus: "we were considered as sheep to be slaughtered"—Rom. 8:36). And Potter, a living metaphor for Satan, is determined to destroy those who have what he wants—he is hardwired to "steal and kill and destroy" (John 10:10). People like George are typically no match for them—they're not expecting to deal with "steal and kill and destroy," and even when they see it coming they don't know what to do about it. Most of us could not stomach picking up the very tools Old Man Potter uses to thwart the evil he intends. George's lack of shrewdness in dealing with Potter almost drives him to suicide, because he's a nice guy, and nice guys don't do shrewd. When the truth about the "game" shrewd people are playing finally dawns on nice people like George and you and me (if it ever does), we are plunged into rage and despair. We suddenly realize we're playing poker with Satan. And that is literally true because, once again, "our struggle is not against flesh and blood, but against the rulers, against the powers, against the world forces of this darkness,

against the spiritual forces of wickedness in the heavenly places"
(Eph. 6:12).

Nice No More

We're disgusted by Old Man Potter. But we're drawn to George
Bailey because he seems so much like the person we want to be—a
gritty, determined, dependable, nice guy. In today's Christian culture, where *nice* is naturally venerated as both the primary evidence
of faith and its primary expression—from our earliest days in Sunday
school right through to the senior ladies quilting circle—*very few of us
do shrewd*. "Conniving" does not fall under any definition of "nice,"
and, therefore, shrewd behavior seems un-Christian. And those scattered few believers who *do* act shrewdly are reluctant to come out of
the closet; they are equally reluctant to pass on to others what they
know. This is why, when Jesus tells us in Matthew 11:12 that the
kingdom of God "suffers violence, and violent men take it by force,"
we scratch our heads, then quickly jump over that verse like it's a
mud puddle. He's saying the kingdom of God is under assault, and
that some kind of force is therefore necessary for advancing it. How
many sermons have you heard on that little enigmatic passage? Zero.

But shrewdness understands exactly what Jesus is saying because
Jesus is speaking its language—there is a hint, maybe an aftertaste,
of violence embedded in shrewd that naturally repels us. Violence
is a strong word, I know, but considered more broadly it's a kind
of forceful momentum that pushes against the current instead of
floating with it—it is willing to push past another's boundaries.

Remember Macaulay's description: "Movement does not simply occur of its own accord, even when you drop something. It needs a driving force."[6] For a moment, lay down your common interpretation of "violence"—a physical assault—and let's define it as "force" instead. In fact, the Greek word translated as "violence" in Matthew 11 is *biazo*, with a literal meaning of "to use force, to apply force to force." Force, then, is at the core of every violent act, when one person intrudes past another's boundaries. And force is what is required when we are advancing a kingdom that is under forceful assault.

We feel this kind of force when we're sitting across from a catbird car salesman as he pounds away on his calculator. *This guy expects me to trust him*, we're thinking, *but I've got to stay on my toes here. I don't want to get taken by him.* We know, intrinsically, that the car salesman wants us to pay more for the car than we'd like to pay. We must counter his force with a little force of our own, because we suspect that our needs and hopes are important to him only as leveraging information. There are few things we hate more than feeling like someone is playing us for the fool. Even more, we abhor the thought that *we* might be playing someone for a fool. That's just not … Christian. Shrewdness is a breach of our social contract with each other—our innate agreement to treat others as we'd like to be treated.

My wife and I go to a chiropractor named Dr. Dennis Nikitow, a wired-for-shrewd man who was honored as US Chiropractor of the Year in 2009.[7] So I decided to study why Dr. Nikitow has been so successful at convincing people like me—who are absolutely, positively opposed to spending the time and money it takes to complete his unorthodox "spinal recovery" program—to go to his office four times a week for at least three months for an intense adjustment regimen. I mean, there was no way I was agreeing to do this—and the next thing I know I'm lying on one of those massage-like tables, waiting for Dr. Nikitow to wrench my head off my shoulders.

One day, as I'm lying on my assigned table, waiting for my wrenching, a man walks in who hasn't been to see Dr. Nikitow for a long time. The office staff greets him like an old friend—"Where've you been?" He, a little sheepish, is equally glad to see them. So he lays himself down on a table at the other end of the room, and Dr. Nikitow comes in and, with a certain sternness, says:

"John, I haven't seen you for a long time—what have you been doing? Have you been busy traveling?"

John, with his head down on the massage table, mumbles as loud as he dares: "Yeah, I've been traveling a lot lately."

"Well, since I haven't seen you for a while, I assumed you weren't motivated to continue with your treatment plan. I took you out of my files." (Do you hear the *force* here?)

The guy grunts his affirmation of the embarrassing truth. Then Nikitow gets to work, interspersing his systematic spinal adjustments with little darts like: "Wow, your lower back is terrible" and "We're going to have to start all over again" and "I don't think they'd let you on a golf course with a back as bad as this."

That last little dart is particularly well-aimed, *thunking* right into the middle of John's weekend passion. Then Nikitow delivers his shrewd coup de grâce: "Are you in today because you're back in the program?" (Again, do you hear the *force* here?)

And John, almost too eagerly, shoots back: "I'm back, yeah, I'm back."

"Well, set up an appointment for a new exam," says a now-conciliatory Nikitow. "I have to see where you're at now that you went off the program." Handing a folder to John, he barks: "Take this to the front, and get an appointment set up for next week."

Then, and only then, Nikitow relaxes a little and smiles as John, still sheepishly, shuffles off to the front office.

This little interchange—carried out in the middle of a bustling office and a captive audience of "fellow travelers"—is a fundamentally forceful interchange. I mean, Dr. Nikitow was committed to pushing past the everyday boundaries we generally maintain in our social and professional relationships, applying force to John's psyche as well as his back. In essence, the way Dr. Nikitow tracked down his wayward "sheep" and prodded him back into the fold was an intrusion—a kind of forceful shove that resulted in John stumbling back into "the program." Remember when Jesus said, in Matthew 18:12, "What do you think? If a man owns a hundred sheep, and one of them wanders away, will he not leave the ninety-nine on the hills and go to look for the one that wandered off?" (NIV)? The sheep wants to wander; the Shepherd wants to find it and bring it back. To the sheep who wants to wander, the Shepherd's rod and staff will feel hard and forceful. But intruding on the sheep's own boundaries to bring it back to safety is a "necessary good." Dr. Nikitow is *fully convinced* that John—and every other person who enters his office—will experience a longer, better life if they will just stick with his program, so he will use the force of shrewd to redirect his "sheep" back to greener pastures.

Of course, it is literally and biblically true that shrewdness is either good or evil, depending on the user's motivation. This is why

Jesus's command to His disciples in Matthew 10 paired the "innocence of doves" with the "shrewdness of snakes."

Moving Sideways on Purpose

This summer my daughter Lucy signed up for a two-week drama camp at a private school a few miles away—apparently, the drama that comes naturally to thirteen-year-old girls can be harnessed, like nuclear fission, and used for the betterment of mankind. So, several days a week I'm Lucy's chauffeur, dropping her off at the front entrance to this private school and picking her up seven hours later. And, I must reveal, I hate doing this for one very simple reason: the private school has created what amounts to an urban obstacle course in an attempt to keep over-busy parents (who always seem late for something) from careening around campus in cars the size of aircraft carriers. There are four daunting speed bumps and a dip that probably qualifies as a ditch between you and the front entrance to the school. What's more, once I've dropped Lucy off, my car is a mere thirty feet away from the entrance road, but I'm not allowed to use that short stretch of pavement to get back on the road because it's supposed to be a one-way street. Instead, school officials (for some reason that I'm sure is aircraft-carrier-related) have set up an elaborate course through the campus that takes me fifty yards away from that entrance road and then loops back on itself to the very point I started from. It's maddening to make this sideways excursion, and therefore, I've brazenly belied the gods of private schools by going the wrong way on that one-way street many times, just because I'm hard-wired to go frontal, not sideways.

My wife responded to my challenge to move more shrewdly with her friend by *honestly* bemoaning the effort it would require—few of us relish the inconvenience of the sideways approach over the more obvious direct route. But shrewd people have made peace with *sideways*, habitually eschewing the frontal approach because they understand how things work. They embrace the truth that sideways is very often the only way to apply the right force at the right time in the right place. Shrewd people are focused on results—they have a challenge in front of them, and they're looking for better, more effective ways to bring redemptive leverage into every situation.

I just got home from a two-hour meeting with a man who owns his own business—I'll call him Max. The other day, when he stopped me in the church hallway to ask for the meeting, there was an urgency in his voice that made my stomach knot up a little. That still, small voice that I'm pretty sure is *not* the Holy Spirit insinuated that I might be walking into an ambush. And I guess it really was kind of an ambush, because Max wanted me to know he was, well …
fed up with the direction things were heading at our church, where I serve as an elder.

Even though I disagreed with Max's overall assessment of "the way things are," I disagreed more deeply with his proposed plan to rectify things. Like most of us in the church, including me, Max assumed the best way to deal with something you disagree with is to counter that *something* directly, with a frontal assault like the US military used so often in World War II but has since abandoned in an age of structurally decentralized enemies that use terrorism as a primary tactic. In this case, Max's direct and frontal approach meant somehow convincing our senior pastor to toe the line and make some radical changes to his ministry vision. I told him that his frontal approach was contingent on the senior pastor fundamentally changing his ministry DNA—the same deeply entrenched convictions that God has repeatedly reaffirmed in him, and the same cultural values that have produced a twenty-year "bumper crop" in the lives of so many. I told him that I didn't think his strategy was going to work, and he might be in danger of smashing against God Himself—if that happened, he'd break into pieces. I asked, "Could I humbly suggest that you reevaluate your trajectory and move more shrewdly instead? I mean, move sideways instead of frontally."

Max tilted his head a little to the side as his eyes narrowed: "What are you talking about?"

That sounded like an open invitation to me, so I leaned in across the table and explained that moving shrewdly means moving sideways, or indirectly, into difficult situations instead of frontally. A frontal approach to the tension he felt is, I think, doomed to failure—you can't force a spiritual leader to morph into the sort of man who's fundamentally contrary to the way God has wired him. I affirmed Max's right to question the direction of the church because of his obvious dissonance with our senior pastor's approach to ministry. But, I said, a shrewd leader would *first* ask God if the proposed "solution" represents a needed course correction or if it is more like venting frustration. If the dissonance is from God, then the frontal approach to resolving it most likely won't work—Max would need to study how things work in the church, then start experimenting with points of leverage that might actually force a shift in the church's culture in the direction he preferred. "You'll find out rather quickly if you're on the right track," I said, "as long as you stay faithful to God as you move."

He squirmed a little in his seat and replied: "Well, I'm still not sure I really understand what you mean by 'shrewd.'" I asked him if he'd ever studied "the one parable you've never heard about in church." Max then pulled out his legal pad and started scribbling notes. "No, what is it, and where is it?"

And so I offered the thumbnail version of Jesus's ridiculously offensive and perplexing story of the shrewd manager, ostensibly directed at His disciples but actually targeted at the "brood of vipers" Pharisees who encircled them. It's nice that we call Jesus the Alpha and the Omega—the Greek words for "the first and the last." But He is also the *Proskomma* and the *Skandalon*, the Greek words translated "rock of offense" and "stone of stumbling" (1 Peter 2:8). Max was still scribbling notes—the effect on me was like throwing chum in the water for a shark—so I bulldozed right into a diatribe about Jesus's parting command to His disciples in Matthew 10. He's sending them out two-by-two on an impossibly daunting mission to "heal the sick, raise the dead, cleanse those who have leprosy, drive out demons" (v. 8 NIV). So He first forbids them to bring along their "conventional" sources of strength and security (money, connections, and resources) and then bluntly tells them that, as a result, they're likely to get eaten alive by enemies who are best described as a ravenous wolf pack. And then, just as He appears to strip them of everything they would need to succeed (blues legend Albert King once observed, "Without bad luck some people would have no luck at all"[8]), Jesus tells His disciples that He won't be sending them out empty-handed. They will need two things—just two "tools"—on their adventure: "Behold, I send you out as sheep in the midst of wolves; so be shrewd as serpents and innocent as doves" (Matt. 10:16).

What would it be like to be one of the disciples, standing there with disbelief and fear clouding your eyes, nervously shifting your weight and stealing furtive glances at the others? It would be very difficult to embrace the reality that the Skandalon Jesus is handing out. His hard and purposefully evasive behavior is impossible to justify, much less understand. He intends to send the disciples off clueless and ill-equipped, offering only the parting advice that they'd better learn, quickly, how to be simultaneously shrewd and innocent. Shrewdness and innocence, He assures, are the only tools "sheep" need to pull off the impossible as they are surrounded and hounded by the immoral and the immutable. Like their Master, Jesus, they will have to live and breathe and move in the midst of their enemies as vipers masquerading as doves.

And, finally, I turned the spigot off my fire hose, and Max stopped scribbling. He smiled at me and did what good men do—he opened himself to change: "You have given me a lot to think about."

The Force of Redemptive Leverage

Ten years ago I joined a nine-week Christian men's group led by a guy who's a professional counselor—I knew very little about him before I signed up for the group, except that he served as a sports chaplain for a couple of local teams. From the first time the group met to the last epic encounter I had with him, this man shattered all my previous templates for Christian social relationships. When we shared stories from our lives that were really thinly veiled excuses to vent our anger and bitterness—the kinds of sympathy-producing stories that are the lifeblood of most men's groups—he made clear his disgust for our subterfuge. When we responded with polite and fearful silence to another man's story, he'd unleash a rocket-launcher diatribe about our passivity and disrespect—our refusal to engage was, bluntly, "cowardice." When I attempted to tell one aspect of my own story with what I proffered up as vulnerability, he agreed with another man that I was like a fog machine—"You're spewing so much smoke in my face that I can't even see you."

By the end of our nine weeks together, half of the guys in the group had retreated into a kind of catatonic silence, and the other half were more alive and awake to God than they'd ever been before. For a variety of reasons, I was in the latter group. But every week I felt as if I were tumbling, like Daniel, into the lion's den—my goal each evening was to resist the urge to curl up like a ball in the corner of the pit and, instead, to stand to face the certain death of his presence.

It's ironic that I *paid* to be a part of this group. But the lesson in shrewdness I learned from this man has turned out to be, simply, priceless.

One night, as the counselor was leaving my home (where we held our meetings), I said something about my wife that seemed to me well within the boundaries of a mild and sociable complaint—a minor frustration, the kind of thing (sorry to admit) men say all the time when their wives or girlfriends aren't around. He turned, opening his bazooka face to me, and said, "I know … your wife's a b****, isn't she?"

The percussion from this explosion was like a deadly wave, and in the split second that followed his remark I was stunned and speechless. I studied his face to see if he was joking or something.

Nope.

The awkward tension of that moment wobbled me—should I be offended or should I take a swing at him or should I let his remark go in or should I ask him to clarify or should I quickly admit that what he was saying was true? I didn't know. And my *not knowing* was a damning exposure of the unconscious darkness of my soul. I managed to stammer: "No, no, no, of course not. I didn't mean it *that* way." His eyes were still boring into me when he replied: "No, I understand—she's a b****. Why don't you just come out and say it?" I stood there awkwardly, searching for even *one word* I could say in response. Nothing.

So he smiled, told me he'd see me next week, and turned to walk away. I stood on our front porch and watched him amble past my wife (who'd stayed away for the evening so we'd have the house to ourselves) as she passed him on our sidewalk. He'd stripped me naked and left me there for public view, producing what must have looked like a ridiculous confusion on my face, because my wife asked me what was wrong. I stammered something about needing to go for a walk—alone, and *right now*....

As I wandered the darkened streets of our neighborhood, I alternately wrestled with indignation and exposure and confusion—in the middle of that, it slowly dawned on me that this guy had merely, accurately, shined a flashlight into a dark place in my soul. He'd simply described the "taste" of my casual condemnation of my wife, then left me reeling in dissonance. His response showed that he'd studied me and that he'd purposefully, strategically, and surgically applied the right force in the right place at the right time. And nothing would ever be the same for me. His *prima facie* summation of my casually brutal attitude toward my wife had smashed a hole in the wall of my prison. Until that moment I had been captive, as many men are, to the twin tyrannies of secrecy and cynicism in my life.

After an hour or so of wandering the empty sidewalks, I finally found my way home, where my wife was waiting for me to explain my erratic behavior. All I could offer her was a chastened heart. I had no coherent explanation for what had just happened to me, but I was braced and determined and energized by my exposure—and that meant I was thirsty for Jesus. At first, and for much of my walk, I hated—*hated*—this guy's response to me. I didn't know it then, but I know it now....

The way this man engaged me was as shrewd as a snake and as innocent as a dove.

It was shrewd because he'd effectively leveraged me, and it was innocent because his motivation was to drive me to repentance. For nine weeks he'd been my worst nightmare, and it was starting to dawn on me that lurking behind his intimidating facade was the light from a beautiful dream—the dream of redemption. His interactions with me always felt like an assault or, at least, a forceful transgression of Christian propriety. So why did I return home that night in the grip of a deeper hope than I'd known before, and worshipping God because of it? The answer is that shrewdness can operate like a powerful lever, knocking us off our guard and opening us to our desperate need for Jesus.

Today, many years later, the shrewd way this man tore down my camouflage, exposing my internal realities, continues to bear beautiful fruit in my life. Because of it, I'm far less likely to hide in the darkness, far more likely to tell the truth, far less likely to play the poser, and much more alert to the way I love my wife. His shrewd assault on my darkness has produced its opposite—a bumper crop of light.

And that's just the kind of impact Jesus, the Sensei of Shrewd, has on people. The reason that Jesus's behavior often seems erratic, counterintuitive, and even incomprehensible to us is that He never says or does anything that isn't shrewd. He is all the time and everywhere leveraging people and situations to His "favored" direction, even (and especially) when He is tender, sensitive, and kind. And He wants us to follow His example—that's why He tells us the Parable of the Shrewd Manager. As His disciples, people who acknowledge the Lordship of Jesus in our lives, our response is to grow as practitioners of shrewd. And if we are *truly* "like sheep running through a wolf pack" (Matt. 10:16 MSG), we ignore His imperative to grow in shrewdness at our own peril.

The glory and the beauty of Jesus is His shocking adherence to the truth at all times, in all situations, with all people. Buried under His obvious disregard for our behavioral sensibilities is His own sly agenda—because He's played poker with Satan and taken him for everything he has, and He wants us to study how he "plays."

Chapter 2

Paths in the Grass

Ignorance is not bliss. Ignorance is poverty. Ignorance
is devastation. Ignorance is tragedy. And ignorance
is illness. It all stems from ignorance.
—Jim Rohn

A dead thing can go with the stream, but only
a living thing can go against it.
—G. K. Chesterton, *The Everlasting Man*

A town in New York asked its construction contractor to build a new
school, but to hold off putting in the sidewalks until they understood
the natural traffic patterns produced by the school's unique layout.
So workers surrounded the school with grass and, for a year, watched
the students and teachers walk across the grass. Only after paths had
already been pounded into the grass did they pour concrete. After

they studied the habit patterns of how people walked on school grounds, they made those patterns permanent by pouring concrete over them.

Like the school's contractors, shrewd people study how things work, then lay down their own "concrete paths" to capitalize on what they've learned. They are *trailblazers* in every sense of the word. And when you're the first person to bushwhack the way from Point A to Point C, you're always much more alive and engaged and attentive than those who will later follow your established paths. The followers can afford to disengage from the landscape and use their "autopilot" to travel the way someone else paid dearly to find. The trailblazer cannot afford this luxury of disengagement. She is scrutinizing the nuances in the landscape, taking risks as she moves into the unknown, failing with regularity, and (finally) making it possible for others to find their way. And this is the transcendent beauty of living more shrewdly—our "concrete paths" make it possible for others to find their way to the hidden treasure in the field, to the pearl of great price, to the mustard seed planted in the garden. When we move more innocently and shrewdly through life, we bring people into the kingdom of God, which is embodied by Jesus Himself:

> Now having been questioned by the Pharisees as
> to when the kingdom of God was coming, He
> answered them and said, "The kingdom of God is
> not coming with signs to be observed; nor will they
> say, 'Look, here it is!' or, 'There it is!' For behold, the
> kingdom of God is in your midst." (Luke 17:20–21)

As we journey more deeply into the kingdom of God, we are becoming more attached to—*more intimately immersed in*—Jesus Himself. And as we do, we learn to behave as He behaves, creating our own concrete paths in the grass. It's good to point out here that trailblazing, just as David Macaulay describes the force necessary to move something or someone toward a favored outcome, "does not simply occur of its own accord."[1] It can be demanding and counterintuitive work.

As I write today I'm near the end of day two of my annual four-day stay at a monastery high in the Colorado Rockies. I come here every year for a short private retreat, staying alone in a small stone "hermitage" on the grounds of St. Benedict's Monastery, which is perched on the back of a horseshoe ridge overlooking what must be one of the most beautiful mountain valleys in the world. Every year I hike up to the top of a small mountain behind the monastery—just to sit on its bald, shale summit and make a cell-phone call to my wife (there's no reception down in the valley). Even though I come here every year, I almost always forget that the trail to the top of this mountain peters out about two-thirds of the way up. That last third can turn into a nightmarish and claustrophobic debacle through thick, cutting underbrush if you don't remember to veer way to the south so you can climb the naked ridge up to the summit. Well, I forgot the way—again—this year. No, "forgot" isn't right—I *chose* the expedience of a direct and treacherous route to the summit rather than the inconvenient, out-of-the-way, and longer sideways route up a gently sloping ridge. The mountain's summit is looming directly in front of you as the trail ends, and it seems crazy to hike another quarter-mile away from the direct route just so you can avoid a hundred yards of eight-foot undergrowth and hike a clear path instead.

So, against the wisdom of past experience, I *trailblazed* through an opening in the underbrush and told myself I'd break through onto the bare shale side of the mountain in no time. Well, it didn't take long to remember why you just don't do that on this hill. I was quickly entangled in thick, impenetrable brush, backtracking and slicing up my legs and arms as I hunted for a way through the maze. I would see openings that promised a path through the mess, crash my way up through the space, then run right into a wall of brambles. I finally made my way through, but only because I launched myself through the smallest of corridors threading like capillaries through the choking maze, finding unseen paths that would've remained hidden had I not taken the risk to explore what didn't seem to be there.

And that's just why my little adventure in ground navigation is such a great parable for taking the first steps in a life that is more proactively shrewd—it's impossible to live it by following a map, or a map's Christian equivalent, biblical principles. No, you find the path as you move into the chaos of your encounters with a commitment to understand how things—people and movements and entities and, at times, underbrush—work. You're not following a script or a linear set of Bible truths. You're following the nudges of a *Person*. And only a *Person* can guide us through the brambles of our chaotic and insensible lives, helping us emerge into the clearing of our calling.

Paying Better Attention

In *Illuminated Life*, Joan Chittister's Benedictine exploration of the contemplative life, she begins a chapter on "Awareness" with this:

"A brother went to see Abba Moses in his hermitage at Scetis and begged him for a word. And the old man said: 'Go and sit in your cell, and your cell will teach you everything.'"[2] Chittister uses this micro-story to expose and challenge our poor track record in paying attention to the people and environments that surround us: "What is right in front of us we see least. We take the plants in the room for granted. We pay no attention to the coming of night. We miss the look of invitation on a neighbor's face…. As a result, we run the risk of coming out of every situation with no more than when we went into it."[3] Here, Chittister is essentially describing why so few of us are skilled, as Jesus is, at understanding how things work. She's writing about a contemplative practice, but she's also unconsciously writing about the tallest hurdle we have to overcome as we enter the training circle of shrewd.

We don't pay attention very well. Sometimes, we don't pay attention at all.

Shrewd people, unlike Chittister's description of the rest of us, never "come out of a situation with less than when [they] went into it." Never. And that's because they're typically not living their lives bouncing from one reaction to the next. They're the accidental contemplatives. They slow down and pay attention to what surrounds them—you have to do that if you're always "studying how things work" and following the lead of a Guide through the chaotic terrain that is your life. And this is why paying attention is the very first conduit for understanding how things work. Again, Chittister writes: "Awareness puts us into contact with the universe. It mines every relationship, unmasks every event, every moment, for the meaning that is under the meaning of it. The question is not so much what is going on in the room, but what is happening to me because of it? What do I see here of God that I could not see otherwise? What is God demanding of my heart as a result of each event, each situation, each person in my life?"[4]

Simply, if we're poor practitioners of proactive awareness, we'll never understand how things work and therefore never learn how to be more shrewd than we are. Socrates reminds us that "an unexamined life is not worth living"—if we're not paying close attention to what motivates others, and what motivates ourselves, we'll never dip below the surface in any relationship, where all the secret mechanizations of life's mysteries live.

One day I was sitting in a grocery store, having lunch with my wife and daughter (actors eat at Spago; editors eat at the grocery store). Two booths away, two teenage guys from the private high school a couple of blocks from the store were acting squirrelly and eating unidentified food wrapped in cellophane. A third guy showed up, triumphantly displaying the coconut he'd just bought and loudly declaring his intention to conquer and eat it. Pause. "Hey, how do you open this thing?" His friends smirked and offered no help. So the guy wandered past me to the plastic utensil bin and carefully selected the sturdiest plastic knife in the pile. Then he proceeded to jam the knife over and over (à la Norman Bates) into the coconut's hairy exterior, to no effect.

"Guys, I can't get this thing open!" Empty stares. So he flagged down a store employee, who shook his head a lot and tried hard to keep from rolling his eyes. Now, for me, this was high drama. Would he conquer the coconut? "The answer on tomorrow's *Dr. Phil.*" Right about then I heard the far-off sound of my daughter's voice—my brain unconsciously registered a "Dad, I'm asking you something" tone. But I didn't hear her. However, I did hear my wife telling her, "Lucy, don't bother Dad right now; he's working."

Well, that statement forced my attention back to my family. I looked at my wife, and she had a matter-of-fact, irony-free look on her face. She'd seen this same scene played out with me hundreds of times. I laughed out loud. She was right—the way people interact, negotiate, and overcome challenges fascinates me. I can't help myself, because I love "understanding how they work." By the time I turned back to the boys, they were squirrelling their way toward the exit, carrying their still-unopened tropical cannon ball. Apparently, round one went to the coconut. I'll never know for sure. I had the vague, frustrated feeling of a guy who missed the last five minutes of a movie.

Those guys will never know it, but I gave them the gift of fascination—I mean, they had my full attention for a brief time. Paying attention is the launching pad for shrewd living, and shrewd living brings freedom to captives. People who pay close attention to others never let tiny revelations float by under the bridge. Most people aren't exactly quick to open themselves for inspection, but they do float a lot of clues our way. And people who are committed to understanding how things work jump on those clues like a fumble in the Super Bowl. Here's a simple example: let's say you run into a friend at the hardware store and ask, "How's it going?" Your friend responds, "Okay, I guess." Already, you have three words that represent a colossal clue to your friend's state of mind. If you do what you normally do, you pretend to take your friend's response at face value and bypass the subtle clue you've been offered. But this time, instead, you follow up that clue by asking, "Why 'okay' and not 'great'?" Whatever you discover in your friend's answer will help you offer something good and useful to him—you'll know what leverage to apply, if any—the right force in the right place at the right time … and for the right reason. But you won't know how to do any of it if you remain in the dark about your friend, if you let his "Okay, I guess" slip by without the pursuit of your attention.

There is a practiced rhythm to paying better attention to people and systems and organizations that is hallmarked by the three habits that we'll explore now.

Habit #1—Asking One More Question

Most of us give up our pursuit of people and systems and institutions much too soon—the truth is always one more question away. Once, when I was walking the leader of my nine-week men's group to the door after our gathering, I asked him if he was headed home. "No, I have a thirty-minute meeting with a man who's really struggling right now." Because I usually felt awkward and self-conscious around this man, I blurted out the only thing that came to mind: "Wow, how much can happen in thirty minutes?" He gave me a half smile and then said, with a kind of casual gravity, "I've found that thirty minutes can change a man's life." With that, he turned and walked out the door. I've thought of that tiny encounter over and over since then, because his response to me was profoundly true. Since then, I've discovered that five minutes—or even one minute—can change a person's life. People are waiting, many of them secretly *wishing*, for someone to unlock them—to understand how they work.

At the end of her farewell show, Oprah Winfrey tried to sum up all that she'd learned about people over the course of her twenty-five-year run hosting the most popular daytime show on tele-vision. With tears in her eyes, she said: "I've talked to nearly thirty thousand people on this show, and all thirty thousand had one thing in common: they all wanted validation. If I could reach through this television and sit on your sofa or sit on a stool in your kitchen right now, I would tell you that every single person you will ever meet shares that common desire. They want to know: 'Do you see me? Do you hear me? Does what I say mean anything to you?'"[5]

It's not as difficult as we assume to play a role in this process of unlocking people, *as long as we're willing to ask one more question than we typically would.*

When I'm invited to speak at conferences, I almost always eat my meals with strangers—I like meeting new people. Not long ago I sat down across from a woman at a table, introduced myself, and asked about her story. She told me she'd recently moved from her longtime home in the upper Midwest to a new church and a new ministry in a new state. She insisted this was all good and she was excited about her new life, but she seemed to *need* to tell me it was all good. Right here—in this moment—is where you and I typically *opt out* from going any deeper. If we're paying attention, we know there's a tone or a certain phrase or a look in the eye that's a clue to what's really going on inside, but we're not sure we have permission to explore, or we're not sure how to go about exploring. We think we have to navigate perfectly, and so we don't navigate at all. I've learned to overcome that barrier by trusting in the latent hunger people have to be explored by someone who values their story.

So I asked this woman what she'd left behind. And, suddenly animated, her eyes lively and bright, she told me about the kids in her former youth group that meant the world to her. In fact, since she and her husband had been unable to have their own children, they'd considered her youth-group kids as their own. I asked her if she now felt "empty nest" syndrome, and she paused … considering her own soul. And then the tears started to come. She admitted her grief and doubt about her new move. Her tears gave me permission to ask one more question. So I asked her if the deeper part of her grief was about her inability to have children of her own. And then the tears accelerated into sobs, right there in the middle of a bustling food court at a convention center. This all happened during the first five minutes of our conversation—her plunging into raw grief at our table and me trying to carry her treasured story gently, like a Fabergé egg. And this is innocent shrewdness at work, helping a woman who needs to grieve find her release in tears.

Living, always, with a commitment to ask "one more question" simply means "launching yourself through the smallest of corridors threading like capillaries through the choking maze, finding unseen paths that would've remained hidden had you not taken the risk to explore what didn't seem to be there." Practically, it means asking *at least* one more follow-up question whenever a person gives you an initial answer to a question:

"How did your mom's surgery go?"

"It went okay, I guess."

"What have been some of your doubts and fears since she was diagnosed?"

"Well, she's telling me everything's going to be okay, but I see the look on her face sometimes, and I'm not so sure."

"So you're not sure you can trust what she's saying to you—has trusting God been difficult for you too?"

This may seem an intrusion on another's boundaries, but that is exactly what innocent shrewdness requires—it's forceful, remember. And, of course, we can easily ask too much or ask badly. But in my decades of pursuing "one more question" with people, I've never—not once—had someone shut down on me. We assume people guard their true selves more diligently than a mama grizzly guards her cubs, but experience tells me that's just not true. People hold back from being more open with us because we refuse to use leverage to pry them open. What I've learned about people has given me the knowledge I need to move more redemptively in their lives. Redemption requires leverage, and you won't gain the leverage you need unless you understand how things work. So, after your next encounter with a friend, pause and ask yourself these two questions:

- "What's one question I was vaguely tempted to ask, but didn't?"
- "Why didn't I ask it?"

Then turn to God for help in answering these questions. Likely, if you're anything like me, the answer will be one of two general responses: (1) "I didn't know what to ask" (representing ignorance, passivity, or laziness), or (2) "I didn't want to be impolite or risk intruding on my friend's boundaries—what if he's offended by my pursuit?" (representing insecurity, fear, or cowardice). Essentially, we're either ignorant in our pursuit of people, or we're afraid to apply force in our relationships, pursuing the clues people give us about themselves and pushing past what we imagine are their well-defended social boundaries to ask the next question. Because we bow to this self-imposed pressure to hold back, we learn very little about what "makes people work." The antidote: in your next encounter, simply determine to act on the nudge you ignored before. Ask at least one more question than you usually would. This, by the way, is a Jesus-like thing to do. The Gospels record Jesus asking 287 questions, many of them the kind of "pursuit" questions that are not easy to answer initially:

- "Which is easier, to say, 'Your sins have been forgiven you,' or to say, 'Get up and walk'?" (Luke 5:23)
- "Why do you look at the speck that is in your brother's eye, but do not notice the log that is in your own eye?" (Luke 6:41)

Also, He loved the leverage that questions produce so much that He often answered questions with questions:

- "Therefore Pilate entered again into the Praetorium, and summoned Jesus and said to Him, 'Are You the King of the Jews?' Jesus answered, 'Are you saying this on your own initiative, or did others tell you about Me?'" (John 18:33–34)

I've always been deeply impacted by something I read years ago in C. S. Lewis's autobiography, *Surprised by Joy*. A turning point in

Lewis's life came when he stepped off a train in Great Bookham, Surrey, as a teenager and met William T. Kirkpatrick (nicknamed "Kirk" or "the Great Knock"), the man his father had engaged as a tutor, who would become the chief architect of Lewis's razor intellect. Nervous about meeting the "tall, very shabbily dressed, ... lean as a rake, and immensely muscular"[6] man, Lewis attempted some awkward conversation:

> I said I was surprised at the "scenery" of Surrey; it
> was much "wilder" than I had expected. "Stop!"
> shouted Kirk with a suddenness that made me jump.
> "What do you mean by wildness and what ground
> had you for not expecting it?"[7]

Quickly, Lewis understood that polite-but-imprecise conversation would have no currency with the Great Knock. This old man who dressed "like a gardener"[8] and conversed like a Weedwacker literally trained Lewis to pay way better attention to his own soul and to the clues those around him were throwing out about themselves. Like taking piano lessons from Mozart, Lewis learned how to make beautiful music with his curiosity, passionately working to "understand how things work" in life and, later, in the kingdom of God.

In an article for the *Christian Century*, pastor Chanon Ross tells how one of his youth-group kids was disgusted by a street preacher screaming fire and brimstone—she didn't like people who were "too religious." Ross asked her what that meant and persisted through her half answers, continuing to ask one more question, until she proclaimed that the screamer was "sort of offensive." Ross replied, "Right, sort of offensive—like when Jesus preached his first sermon and made everyone so mad they tried to kill him?" That shrewd question-response threw the girl into "a storm of mental dissonance—the hard thinking that precedes theological insight."[9] Because he persisted in his pursuit of the girl, asking successive questions so he could better understand how her mental processes worked, he knew how to apply the right force in the right place at the right time to bring about the sort of dissonance that leads to a deeper embrace of truth and a more intimate relationship with Jesus. This is why asking one more question is a crucial pursuit in "understanding how things work." If Lewis were still with us, he'd be raising a pint to the "storm of mental dissonance" that "hard thinking" produces when we ask the next question.

Habit #2—Thinking Like Sherlock Holmes

In an eight-hour experience I lead called "The Jesus-Centered Life," I have people do something with each other that's highly risky—in fact, this particular exercise is the riskiest thing I've ever done with people in a training setting. And that's saying something, because everything I do is experiential and interactive and therefore uncomfortable (at least initially) for most people. First, I show them a four-minute clip from the classic PBS series *Sherlock Holmes*, starring Jeremy Brett with Edward Hardwicke as Watson. In the scene, Holmes and Watson are studying a bowler hat that was left at the scene of a mysterious incident—it is their only clue to the mystery. Holmes proclaims, in his enjoyably egotistical way, that everything they need to know about the man who was wearing the bowler hat can be discovered just by studying it. He challenges Watson to examine the hat and offer his theories. Watson, incredulous and dismissive, quickly gives the hat his once-over and proclaims the task hopeless. Holmes picks up the hat, studies it, then tells Watson that it belongs to a well-to-do man who's fallen on hard times. This man has a great deal of self-respect, is of better-than-average intellect, is overweight and out of shape, is married to a woman whose love for him has cooled, and no longer uses "gas lighting" at his home, preferring candles instead.

At this point Watson bursts out laughing at Holmes's hubris, daring him to prove each of his wacky assertions. And Holmes carefully points out:

- The hat was expensive—"of the highest quality"— when it was new, but it has since descended into shabbiness, thus proving his "formerly well-to-do" observation and his assertion that the man's wife has cooled in her love for him because she is no longer taking care of the hat for him,
- The sweat-soaked band inside the hat proves his "overweight and out of shape" observation,
- Its wide circumference, says Holmes, suggests a large brain capacity,
- The slight wax stains on the top of the hat show that the man's home is lit by candles, not the more expensive gas lanterns, and
- The hat has the remnants of expensive accessories on it, but they are broken and have not been replaced—underscoring the idea that he was once well off but is not any longer.

Watson, though he has seen this sort of thing before, reacts with open-mouthed amazement. End of scene.[10]

I then ask people what they observed in the scene that gives clues to Holmes's genius. They talk about his peculiar attention to detail and his insightful deductions as a result. Then I ask them to form a small group with two other people and arrange their chairs so they're facing each other. Then I tell trios I'm going to give them each three minutes to study at least one other person in their group and, just as Holmes did with the bowler hat, make educated deductions about that person. For example, if a guy is wearing TOMS shoes, you might deduce that he's the sort of person who is cause-driven, because TOMS is a cause-driven company (an actual and true observation from this exercise). They are to observe as many details as they can, then write down their assumptions. I tell them that it will be tempting to talk or to laugh to break the tension of those three minutes, but that they are to be silent through it all. After three minutes of agony, I ask groups to share what they've written down about each other. I give them a few minutes for this, then I ask people to raise their hands if they heard something true about themselves that surprised them. Always, hands go up all over the room. And the open-mouthed-in-amazement stories flow. People are stunned when they realize the power of passionate attention to detail.

Shrewd people are peculiar in that they have an abnormal affinity for detail, allowing them to make reasoned assumptions about people that are most often in the ballpark. And because they understand more fully than others the unique patterns and eccentricities and motivations of the people around them, their knowledge allows them to apply the right force in the right place at the right time.

Passionate pursuers are always thinking one step ahead of the pursued, always trying to unlock that person's reality. Think of the people around you as mysteries you're trying to solve. Challenge yourself to enter into every conversation with a mission to pay attention to people more acutely than the rest of humanity does. This is how we *gain information* about people in every situation. Instead of merely listening to people, study them. It's as simple as noticing when one of your chatty friends is uncharacteristically quiet, then asking her what's been happening at home lately. Pay way more attention to details than you have before, then follow your gut and ask a question based on what you observe or sense.

I once spent an hour in a van with a seventeen-year-old student named Trevor—we had both endured several hours on a plane and were now on our way to a huge gathering of Christian teenagers at a Bible college in rural Canada. I spent about forty minutes of that hour asking Trevor questions. When I asked him why he traveled so far to attend the event, he told me he used to go to the Christian high school that's attached to the college, and he was looking forward to seeing his friends again. He left school before finishing his final year because he had an "incredible" job opportunity in the oil industry. No, he had no regrets about leaving early because he was making "really good money."

Well, "good money" seemed like the answer he thought he was supposed to give me, so I asked if there was any other reason he left school. "Well," he told me, "I don't get along well with my parents." When I asked why, he thought for a while, then said, "They just have different morals than me." So I asked, "Are yours better or worse than theirs?" He then described his parents as ultra-conservative

Christians who were unrealistic and inflexible. So Trevor missed his friends at school and had a strained relationship with his parents, and now he was living hundreds of miles away on his own. The key to understanding Trevor, I thought, was unlocking the real emotions behind his decision to leave school. So I asked him what his "incredible" job involved. Basically, he spent his day measuring fuel in tanks and selling knickknacks at a commercial fuel outpost.

This was an intelligent, ambitious kid, and the details of his job didn't match his enthusiasm for it. But he was determined to make me believe he was happy because to admit his unhappiness would mean exposing himself in a way he couldn't afford to do. He was trying as hard as he could to make the best of his situation, and to reveal his true feelings would sabotage his resolve. So, because I'm learning how to be a peculiar person who's "always thinking one step ahead of the pursued, always trying to unlock that person's reality," I asked more questions and discovered that Trevor lived in an apartment with his older brother, who was seriously disabled by a "mystery ailment." As a result, his brother who had once loved God now hated Him. This massive truth that remained hidden under several layers of polite conversation told me Trevor was likely desperate to be reminded of God's goodness and was longing for the Christian fellowship and environment he once took for granted. As the van pulled up to my little hotel, this is the truth I knew about Trevor: he'd never wanted to leave school in the first place, he missed his friends and his relationship with God, and he had traveled halfway across Canada hoping to find hope in God again. My "peculiar attention to detail" followed by pursuing questions helped surface his aching, lonely, hungry heart—our encounter helped flush out of hiding his desperate need for God.

We meet people every day who spew clues for us to pursue, but we typically don't. Someone says something (or doesn't say something) that makes us think there's a story behind there somewhere. But all we see is a bowler hat, and so we (like Watson) give only cursory attention to the clues that would be perfectly obvious to a person who's paying attention (like Holmes). And the truth is, no one in history has paid more peculiar attention to people than Jesus. But because we know Jesus is God, we make a fundamental assumption that He used His "superpowers" all the time in His sojourn on earth. However, Jesus is also man, and some of the amazing things He did were, clearly, because He paid peculiar attention to people so He could understand how they work. For example, let's explore the well-known story of Jesus engaging "the woman at the well" in John 4:

> There came a woman of Samaria to draw water. Jesus
> said to her, "Give Me a drink." For His disciples
> had gone away into the city to buy food. Therefore
> the Samaritan woman said to Him, "How is it that
> You, being a Jew, ask me for a drink since I am a
> Samaritan woman?" (For Jews have no dealings with
> Samaritans.) Jesus answered and said to her, "If you
> knew the gift of God, and who it is who says to you,
> 'Give Me a drink,' you would have asked Him, and
> He would have given you living water." She said to
> Him, "Sir, You have nothing to draw with and the
> well is deep; where then do You get that living water?
> You are not greater than our father Jacob, are You,

who gave us the well, and drank of it himself and his sons and his cattle?" Jesus answered and said to her, "Everyone who drinks of this water will thirst again; but whoever drinks of the water that I will give him shall never thirst; but the water that I will give him will become in him a well of water springing up to eternal life."

The woman said to Him, "Sir, give me this water, so I will not be thirsty nor come all the way here to draw." He said to her, "Go, call your husband and come here." The woman answered and said, "I have no husband." Jesus said to her, "You have correctly said, 'I have no husband'; for you have had five husbands, and the one whom you now have is not your husband; this you have said truly." The woman said to Him, "Sir, I perceive that You are a prophet.... I know that Messiah is coming (He who is called Christ); when that One comes, He will declare all things to us." Jesus said to her, "I who speak to you am He."

At this point His disciples came, and they were amazed that He had been speaking with a woman, yet no one said, "What do You seek?" or, "Why do You speak with her?" So the woman left her waterpot, and went into the city and said to the men, "Come, see a man who told me all the things that I have done; this is not the Christ, is it?" (vv. 7–29)

There are patterns and tones and echoes of Sherlock Holmes studying the bowler hat in this little interchange. The woman at the well is asking questions that reveal something about her. Jesus is studying her. Is He using some kind of supernatural mind-reading ability? Or is He paying peculiar attention to the details—the hints and clues and nuances—that she is projecting, then proving He understands how she works by repeating back to her "all the things that I have done"? My money's on the latter explanation. Jesus is both God and man, and that means the way He relates with people is a mix of the infinite and the finite—this is the way the Trinity wants it. So, it makes sense that He would not habitually operate in the infinite (mind-reading everyone He meets) and, instead, often operate in the finite (paying peculiar attention to details). Because He is urging us—through His last-minute instructions to His disciples in Matthew 10 and through the Parable of the Shrewd Manager—to think and act shrewdly, it makes perfect sense that He would always be practicing what He preaches. I think Jesus delights in "unlocking" people like the woman at the well, because He delights in using the leverage of shrewd to redeem people and set them free from their captivity.

Habit #3—Pursuing with Persistence

Passionate pursuers—people who are committed to understanding how things work—are driven by their own curiosity. They don't give up. And the people and institutions and systems they're pursuing soon learn that truth and feel leveraged by it. Everyone has his or her own personal "push away" strategy that challenges pursuers to show how serious they are. And every one of these people has a tipping point that, once reached, opens the floodgates.

In the movie *The Horse Whisperer* (based on the true story of horse trainer Buck Brannaman), Robert Redford plays Tom Booker, a cowboy renowned for his ability to work with difficult horses. He's not a horse psychologist—he just *sees* them well because he pays peculiar attention to them. He understands the leverage his own painful past has exerted on his heart, and, therefore, he can reach the painful places that are fueling a horse's damaging behavior. In the film's pivotal scene, Tom is trying to break through with Pilgrim, a horse badly injured after a logging truck slams into him.

The accident almost kills Pilgrim's owner and rider, fourteen-year-old Grace. Doctors had to amputate her leg, and she's been in a deep depression ever since. Meanwhile, Pilgrim is disfigured and emotionally unstable—the veterinarians advise Annie, Grace's mom, to destroy the horse. Annie, traumatized by the accident, refuses. So Pilgrim lives in the limbo between life and death—too injured, angry, and afraid to be ridden, but not so damaged that he can't eat, sleep, and … exist. Annie loads the horse in a trailer and takes off with her daughter to Montana to convince Tom, a renowned "horse whisperer" who has an uncanny ability to unlock problem horses, to work with Pilgrim.

Once he agrees to Annie's request, Tom attempts to do what others could not—reach past Pilgrim's violent defense mechanisms to calm his fears and heal his wounds. Soon after he begins working with Pilgrim, the horse lashes out at Tom, knocking him down. Pilgrim gallops off into a vast meadow. The onlookers, including Annie and Grace, gasp as the furious horse disappears into a sea of long grass. But Tom picks himself up, walks silently past Grace and Annie into the meadow, then hunkers down in the grass to wait on the horse. Calmly, he kneels and stares at the horse in the distance—not for a few minutes, *but the entire day*. By dusk, the horse has seen enough. He slowly ambles toward Tom, finally allowing him to stroke his nose and walk him back to the ranch.[11]

This is a story of breakthrough—not just for the horse, but for its teenage owner, who is just as broken. Tom's persistent pursuit, going way beyond what others would do, brings freedom to captives. His persistence is itself a force that others must reckon with. And Pilgrim is a perfect symbol for many of us—wounded, afraid, and lonely, he's constructed walls around his broken places, making it daunting for those around him to see past his abrasive, distancing behavior and touch his soul. But in our hyper-speed world, who has the time to wait on a hurting person? The ones who are willing to persist over time win the day. The hidden imperative here is that we all need someone to commit to us long enough to outlast all our "push away" protective tricks. Shrewd people are persistent in their pursuit because they know "lost sheep" are hoping against hope that they'll one day meet someone like Jesus, who spends all His time passionately hunting down lost coins, lost sheep, and lost sons and daughters. He is a persistent pursuer by His very nature. And the only hope the captives around us have is running into someone who acts like Jesus.

In general, we suffer from a terminal lack of persistent curiosity about our most compelling mysteries—the stories of the people around us. We're drawn to powerful stories, but we often don't recognize them buried under the "push away" strategies of those who fill up the mural of our lives. We celebrate the life stories we see in the Bible, but forget that God is writing every person's story, not just David's, Solomon's, or

Paul's. We have proved we can be relentless in our pursuit—we have a host of magazines, TV shows, tabloid newspapers, websites, radio programs, smartphone apps, and books that illustrate the lengths of our persistence when it comes to the stories of celebrities. We can't suppress our hunger for life stories—we simply satisfy that hunger through voyeurism. Longtime family counselor Royce Frazier tells parents that the key to living well is simply spending "curious time" with their kids.[12] But most kids believe it's easy to fool adults, because adults aren't often persistently curious about kids' lives and therefore have no idea of who they are or what their reality is like.

If we hope to understand how things work with people and institutions, we will have to be persistent. Remember Dr. Sharp's advice: "If you're living under a dictator, you really have to know that particular system extremely well." And knowing anything extremely well will require a tenacious spirit. Persistent pursuers are continually asking themselves these questions when they engage people:

- "Would this person say I'm riveted by him/her in this moment?"
- "What interior and exterior distractions do I need to set aside to rivet my attention right now?"

Living Sweet-ly

After a particularly demanding season of my life, when my approach to everyone and everything had devolved into serial reactivity, my good and wise friend Bob Krulish wrote me this note:

Rick, I know Thursday's are not good days for you,
but I go down to the Mt. St. Francis retreat center
north of Colorado Springs each month for "a day
away with the Lord." Usually some elders and staff
go as well, and I would love to have you join us. If
you can't come with us, I sure would encourage you
to put it on your schedule—at a time that would
fit you. You are wired to hear from the Lord, and
stopping everything for a day would catapult you in
terms of intimacy. Just a thought and offer![13]

Here, Bob is challenging me to get past reactionary living and
become more aware of the "plants in the room"—to live my life
intentionally by paying attention to what's motivating God's heart,
what's motivating my own soul, and what is going on in others. He
is asking me to do what it takes to "understand how things work,"
in my own heart and in the hearts of others. Dr. Rachel Remen,
founder of the Institute for the Study of Health and Illness, writes:
"Real stories take time. We stopped telling stories when we started to
lose that sort of time, pausing time, reflecting time, wondering time.
Life rushes us along and few people are strong enough to stop on
their own. Most often, something unforeseen stops us and it is only
then we have the time to take a seat."[14]

I crave this way of attentive living, because I know that shrewd
living requires it. Shrewd living is, I think, just another way of describing what it looks like to follow Jesus into His redemptive mission.
And no one I've ever met exemplifies that more than Leonard Sweet,
a prolific author, preacher, futurist, and professor of evangelism at

Drew Theological School. Over the course of more than two decades as editor of *Group Magazine*, I've interviewed Len multiple times and connected with him at conferences and at our headquarters. He, like the contractors who studied the paths in the grass before they laid down concrete sidewalks, is driven by a passion to understand how things work, then use that knowledge for redemptive leverage. You'll see what I mean in this short interchange from one of our recorded conversations:

> **Me:** When you think about what's urgent regarding the church's future direction, what has immediate application to ministering to young people?

> **Sweet:** First of all, I really have problems with that whole term *youth ministry*. I think it has a musty smell to it. I look at myself as being in mid-youth. Middle age is now thirty-eight to eighty. So I have definitional problems with the language the church is using to talk about one of its most important missions—to pass the baton of faith from one generation to another.

> **Me:** Have you thought of good alternatives?

> **Sweet:** We should be using the language of generational cultures. What "youth ministry" suggests is that youth is a fixed category that doesn't change over time. But we've got at least five, six, sometimes

even seven generational cultures that we're dealing with. Boomer youth were different than Gen X youth, who are different than NetGen youth. The question is, "What are the peculiar characteristics of this generational culture with which I'm entrusted?" And that culture is going to change every five or six years. To do this kind of generational ministry, we must keep ahead of the curves—to keep updated, to keep going to conferences, to keep learning, to keep listening.

Me: What you're saying is that the term *youth ministry* assumes "youth" is the same from generation to generation, and that creates a kind of bulwark against change for youth ministers.

Sweet: Right.

Me: So what kind of training or preparation for change would you recommend for a youth minister today?

Sweet: One is that you tailor your learning to the context. So you look at what NetGens like to do most, for example. Their favorite pastime is [watching] movies, their second favorite pastime is [social media]. Well, immediately that tells me something. If you do not understand that film has been the major cultural dynamic of the twentieth century, and you are not constantly learning and getting film and media savvy, you cannot communicate to this generation. Secondly, if you have no idea what online life is about—if you only have an offline life—you do not know that, for this generation, the Internet is their soda fountain or their water cooler. These kids are saying to us: "You want to communicate with us? You want to speak our language? You gotta know about film and the Net."

Me: I see youth ministers leaning into two broad camps. One camp dips into the waters of kids' culture because they have a compelling desire to understand and connect with them. These people are seen as somewhat dangerous by the church.

Sweet: Well, there's no understanding without standing under. And that's what these people are willing to do. They're saying, "To understand these kids, we gotta stand under their culture."[15]

Understanding how things work means we will have to, as Sweet so artfully reveals, commit ourselves to "standing under." And when we stand under people or institutions or our own souls, we are acting like the trailblazers God created us to be, shrewdly finding our way forward in the choking maze that is, often, our everyday life.

Chapter 3

Dancing the Tango

To act on the light one has is almost the only way to more light.
—C. S. Lewis, *Yours, Jack*

If you were given an impossible task with no resources, do you think you're going to get the job done by following all the rules? No.
—Chris Stanton, missionary and author of *The Quiet Evolution*

Not long ago, after my friend and pastor Tom Melton used a video of two people dancing the tango as an illustration in a sermon, he received an email from a woman in our congregation named Emily Wurtzbacher. This is what she wrote:

> As a competitive ballroom dancer, I love the tango and have an interesting story for you about when I was learning it. When my partner was teaching me how to

tango he showed me the position and then asked me
to close my eyes. When I did, we started dancing all
around the floor. It felt like I had been doing it for years
and I knew exactly what I was doing—I soon realized,
though, that once I felt like I could do it on my own
and I didn't follow him or didn't put as much of my
weight on him, I got lost. So lost. We would trip over
each other and have to stop dancing completely. After
our first full tango he stopped and told me to open
my eyes. He asked if my dad and I were close. I said
yes, and asked him why. He said that he figured my
dad and I were close because I didn't have a problem
trusting him. Then I closed my eyes with no problem
and followed him (for the most part) very well. He told
me that a lot of people who try to learn the tango aren't
very successful because they can't follow the man. They
can't trust him. That got me thinking not only about
how great my daddy is, but also how great God is. How
cool is it that I can dance through life smoothly if, and
only if, I follow Him? If I lean on Him and let Him
lead me. The second I start to pull away or try to do
things my way I stumble. What a great security knowing that my Partner is always there; all I have to do is
lean in and let Him sweep me away.[1]

Just as the "Arab Spring" (the nonviolent revolutions that resulted
in democratic reforms throughout the region) in early 2011 was not
the result of a linear progression of strategic decisions with predictable

outcomes, our commitment to understand how things work can sound like a linear mental process but is actually more like dancing the tango. We're delightfully reduced to a dependent relationship with God as we pay better attention to the people and institutions that fill up our lives, then use that knowledge to experiment with redemptive leverage. As we set off to live more shrewdly than we are living now, our senses are awake and alert and searching the void for clues to the hidden openings that mark the path ahead. And this means we're in a *dependent relationship* with our Guide—just the way He likes it. And so we launch ourselves into the openings and fissures in the brambles in front of us, adjusting our course with every new bit of information, looking for the light and depending on Jesus moment to moment. We are committed to understanding how things work, so we are continuously learning—and we are always and everywhere paying closer attention to our Teacher, following His lead with our eyes closed.

I love what author John Eldredge says about the difference between following principles (a road map) and following Jesus (the Guide) in his book *Waking the Dead*. After retelling the Tolkien story from *The Fellowship of the Ring* of how the ranger Strider (later the crowned king Aragorn) leads four small hobbits through a maze of back roads and hidden trails to throw off their deadly Nazgûl pursuers, Eldredge makes a profound statement: "If you're not pursuing a dangerous quest with your life, well, then, you don't need a Guide. If you haven't found yourself in the midst of a ferocious war, then you won't need a seasoned Captain."[2]

If you live shrewdly, you'll need a Guide and a Captain at every turn because shrewd-for-good people don't follow scripts or principles or formulas—*they follow Jesus* into His dangerous rescue mission, advancing His kingdom (therefore, advancing *Him*) while evading the wickedness that pursues them. In that sense, you're not really living if you're not living shrewd. The shrewd life is a life awake—a life of adventure and risk and intimacy. And all real adventures are dangerous; that's what *makes* them adventures. If you think about it, all the adventures you've ever experienced have been dangerous because, at least, they've wrested control from you. If you're always in control, you're not really on an adventure. Lack of control makes us uncomfortably dependent. "Understanding how things work" is a fundamentally dependent activity, because we cannot understand on our own. We need a Master who will take the lead in the tango— Jesus Himself.

Our adventures in the land of shrewd will certainly force us into a dependent relationship with our Guide—and it's this dependent relationship that the Guide is *really* after. He *wants* us to close our eyes when we dance the tango with Him. We have our goals in life, and we are already finding ways to leverage the people and things around us to inch our way closer to them. But God's only goal is our redemption, leading to a restored (dependent) relationship with Him that is characterized by freedom and intimacy. And so, the Sensei of Shrewd is always drawing all of us to Himself (John 12:32)—at all times and everywhere using His knowledge about our ways to leverage our circumstances and our relationships to woo us.

Jesus wants us to live shrewdly, and do it innocently, because He is shrewd and innocent—He's our quintessential example for "studying how things work." He knows the advance of His kingdom requires dependent brothers and sisters summoning the courage to learn as they go, leveraging every situation for the kingdom of God because they are infected with the Spirit of Jesus.

The Oblique Approach

Teaching people to live their lives by following a cascading set of biblical imperatives seems like the most direct path to maturity in Christ. But the direct path is often overrated and surprisingly counterproductive. A more shrewdly oblique path, in both our life with Christ and in geography, leads to true breakthrough. For example, the most direct east-to-west crossing of the American continent, bridging from the Atlantic to the Pacific, would go through Nicaragua. But the waterway that allows ships to cut months off of their journey from east to west was built, instead, at a more shrewdly oblique angle across Panama that starts in Colon and ends in Balboa—when the journey through the Panama Canal is complete, ships actually end up thirty miles *east* of where they started. But, it turns out, the direct route through Nicaragua is a lot longer than the oblique route through Panama. Oxford's famed professor of economics, John Kay, calls this approach to pursuing our life's objectives "obliquity."[3] The oblique approach means, simply, pursuing a slanted or indirect strategy instead of a direct approach.[4] It's moving sideways instead of frontally.

Direct paths, in geography and in our spiritual life, most often require greater and greater determination and willpower to succeed. That's why Jesus hardly ever "shoulds" on people by telling them to simply try harder in their efforts to "keep the Law" in their lives. Far from that, He essentially tells us we have no hope of crafting our own version of righteousness (Matt. 5:20). Instead, He offers an oblique solution to our problem—He will simply exchange His righteousness for the "filthy rags" of our willful efforts to maintain our goodness.

The beauty of "obliquity" is also embedded in Jesus's preferred teaching method—the indirect use of storytelling, conversational interaction, and learning by experience instead of the more direct and principle-based strategy of didactic lecture. The University of British Columbia's Carl Wieman, a Noble-Prize winner and science adviser to President Barack Obama, found that in nearly identical classes, Canadian college students learned a lot more from young teaching assistants using interactive methods than they did from a veteran professor giving a traditional lecture. The students who used "clicker" devices to interact with their lesson did twice as well on a test, compared to those who heard the "highly rated veteran professor" lecture about the topic. Students in the interactive class-room got little or no lecturing—instead, they participated in short discussions in small groups, responded to in-the-moment "clicker" quizzes, learned from thematic experiences, and dialogued in question-and-answer sessions. Lloyd Armstrong, the former provost at the University of Southern California and a professor of physics and education, agreed that the study shows "it's not the professor, it's not even the technology, it's the approach."[5]

And the approach Armstrong is referencing is oblique, just as Jesus's teaching is almost always oblique—just as a shrewd way of living and interacting is oblique. Not coincidentally, dancing the tango is an oblique art form, as opposed to dancing the waltz, which is more of a linear art form. The tango was born in the brothels of Argentina and is a free-form style of dance—great tango dancers respond to nuances in each other, rather than following a prescribed series of steps. Translating the tango into the broader language of life, John Kay writes: "The process in which well-defined and prioritized objectives are broken down into specific states and actions whose progress can be monitored and measured [like the waltz] is not the reality of how people find fulfillment in their lives, create great art, establish great societies or build good businesses."[6] Anecdotally, it's easy to find examples that support Kay's "greatness through obliquity" dictum:

- A college degree is universally acknowledged as a direct route to career success, but Bill Gates took the oblique route, dropping out of Harvard at age twenty to launch a little business called Microsoft. In the decade that followed, he became the first person in history to earn billionaire status by age thirty.

- When Scott Joplin was a child in early twentieth-century Texas, his father, Giles, left his mother, Florence, for another woman. One source of tension in their marriage came from Florence's insistence on continuing to support her son's music education—Giles didn't believe Scott could ever earn a decent living as a musician. The most direct way to earn income for the family, contended Giles, was to get his son working as early as possible as a laborer.[7] But, instead, Scott's mom was adamant about the oblique path of a career in music, and he later adopted and refined a new style of music called ragtime. His composition "Maple Leaf Rag" was one of the best-selling songs of his time,[8] and, much later, his compositions eventually won an Academy Award for the soundtrack to the film *The Sting*.[9] That year Joplin's song "The Entertainer" won a Grammy for Marvin Hamlisch.[10]

• Early in its long run on public television, the producers of *Sesame Street* decided to heed the conventional (and frontal) advice of child psychologists and ban the show's human actors from interacting with the Muppets—the professionals were worried that kids would feel confused and misled by these cross-species relationships. When the Children's Television Workshop tested the new format, they found kids paid attention to the show when the Muppets were on the screen but lost interest when only the human actors were on the screen. So the producers ditched the recommended advice and decided to use an oblique—and conventionally confusing—approach that later became a central facet of the show's success. The solution? Have Jim Henson build Muppets big enough to interact with full-sized humans—and that's how we got Big Bird and Oscar the Grouch, among others. More than 77 million adults have grown up watching the show, and *Sesame Street* has won a record 118 Emmy Awards.[11]

- John Stuart Mill, a British philosopher who
  was later one of the fathers of modern social-
  economic theory and a huge influence in the
  spread of democracy as a politically superior way
  to govern, escaped his own prison of depression
  when he decided that, essentially, he could not
  find happiness by making it the direct goal of
  his life, but instead by fixing his mind on some
  other pursuit.[12] This is a prime example of Kay's
  overarching assessment that great financial and
  social success is a by-product, not a direct aim,
  of pursuing a worthwhile mission in life. Kay is a
  tango man, not a waltz man.

Jesus was always telling unforgettable "tango" stories that had no "moral," per se (that's why His disciples were most often confused by them)—instead, the stories revealed the central values and persistent "norms" of God's kingdom. For example, the parable of the mustard seed in Matthew 13:31–32: "The kingdom of heaven is like a mustard seed, which a man took and sowed in his field; and this is smaller than all other seeds, but when it is full grown, it is larger than the garden plants and becomes a tree, so that the birds of the air come and nest in its branches." There's no definable moral to this story, but there is a definable "central value and persistent norm" that is intrinsic to God's kingdom: tiny things are all the time growing into enormous things that offer sanctuary.

Professor Kay would call these persistent norms "high-level objectives." Writing about Franklin Roosevelt, Kay says he "is admired today because he achieved [his] high-level objectives, but he did so through pragmatic improvisation in the face of circumstances that neither he nor his outstanding advisers could predict or control."[13] God's intention is to plant these norms—or the high-level objectives of the kingdom of God—in our souls, like seeds that grow into oak trees in our lives. Then He expects us to live out of these high-level objectives in an improvisational, tango-like way. Paul is describing this way of living his life for Christ when he writes, "But to me it is a very small thing that I may be examined by you, or by any human court; in fact, I do not even examine myself. For I am conscious of nothing against myself, yet I am not by this acquitted; but the one who examines me is the Lord" (1 Cor. 4:3–4). He's saying, essentially, that he's not always checking himself to see if he's living according to the rules (a frontal adherence to the Law)—instead, he lives his life pursuing the "high-level objectives" of the kingdom of God and trusts the Spirit of God living in him to alter his trajectory, if necessary.

The oblique approach to teaching described in the New Testament is the answer to "What Would Jesus Do?" The examples of principle-based teaching in Jesus's ministry are few (the Beatitudes, for example), while the examples of oblique teaching are many (the fifty-five parables He tells, and the many debates He engages in with His disciples and the Pharisees, not to mention the times He asks His disciples to walk on water or cast out demons or catch fish that have coins in their mouths). Jesus is a subversive—over and over He prods the people of His time to think differently about the "givens" in their culture. He does this by approaching problems and people obliquely—His goal is to spur His followers to engage their cultural "truths," not run from them or sponge from them, and to confound those who have evil intent toward Him unless their actions play into His own intentions. Luke records one such story:

> One day He was teaching; and there were some Pharisees and teachers of the law sitting there, who had come from every village of Galilee and Judea and from Jerusalem; and the power of the Lord was present for Him to perform healing. And some men were carrying on a bed a man who was paralyzed; and they were trying to bring him in and to set him down in front of Him. But not finding any way to bring him in because of the crowd, they went up on the roof and let him down through the tiles with his stretcher, into the middle of the crowd, in front of Jesus. Seeing their faith, He said, "Friend, your sins are forgiven you." The scribes and the Pharisees began to reason, saying, "Who is this man who speaks blasphemies? Who can forgive sins, but God alone?" But Jesus, aware of their reasonings, answered and said to them, "Why are you reasoning in your hearts? Which is easier, to say, 'Your sins have been forgiven you,' or to say, 'Get up and walk'?" (Luke 5:17–23)

Here Jesus avoids a direct response to the Pharisees (*"Who is this man? Well, I'm the Son of God—did you miss that lesson in Sunday school?"*) and instead offers them a shrewd and therefore oblique response that's like a worm eating its way into their hearts. Obliquity is why Jesus so often began His teaching sessions with His disciples by saying, "You have heard it said …" Then He'd proceed to restate a commonly accepted cultural "truth" ("You shall love your neighbor and hate your enemy"—Matt. 5:43) followed by a push-back with a kingdom-of-God truth ("But I say to you, love your enemies and pray for those who persecute you"—v. 44). Because He understands that dissonance is a powerful force in our lives, Jesus repeatedly creates dissonance in both friend and foe—the point is to leverage people by studying them, then surprise them with what He says and does.

The Face of Obliquity

The other day I was listening to a story on the radio about Los Angeles's chronic gang problem and how community leaders and police are cracking down on gang leaders. Embedded in the report was a story about the death of longtime "gang interventionist" Lilly Rodriguez. She was a former kickboxing champion who gave her life, literally, to helping extract teenagers from "la vida loca"—the crazy gang lifestyle. At her funeral, a reporter talked to Gilbert Alvarado, one among thousands who showed up to honor Rodriguez. "I met her about 10 years ago, when I was a little kid running around in the streets," Alvarado said. "She just changed my life. She really did. Man, she helped a lot of guys like me in gangs. She'd teach them boxing as a way out of the gangs. 'C'mon,' she said, 'I'll show you how to fight.' To her last day, she was trying to help me out. 'Gilbert,' she said, 'I believe in you, mi'jo.' I never had nobody show me that affection, that love." Alvarado wept as he spoke these words. If Rodriguez had tried to rescue him from his gang lifestyle with a more direct approach, he likely would've ignored her. But because she chose the more oblique and shrewd approach, teaching "boxing as a way out of the gangs," Alvarado's life was changed forever.[14]

For years and years I've studied the experiences in teenagers' lives that lead to true and lasting connection within Christian communities. My favorite story of "lasting connection" appeared in an old column we used to run called Strange But True. I titled youth pastor Eric Robinson's story "The Atomic Woodchuck"—it's a quintessential example of how we don't always "catch" the learning intended by those who are leading us and, instead, glom on to alternate, and oblique, lessons:

> Our youth group had spent three days camping on islands in the Allegheny River. On the way home, we cruised along a country highway, talking about the adventures we'd had canoeing, swimming, and poking sticks at things. It was still hot out, and the windows were open, so we had to reminisce above the roar of the wind. Suddenly, just ahead of me in the oncoming lane, I noticed one truck—and then another—swerve abruptly in the road. As a third vehicle barreled toward us, it chose to drive through the obstruction, rather than around it. And considering that the object was merely a dead woodchuck and the vehicle was a pickup truck, it was obvious that the road kill would have to give.

The girls in back giggled about something. Time seemed to stand still. The windows were open … something in my head told me to duck. (People say that in times of crisis adrenaline can give you almost superhuman abilities. It may not have been superhuman, but I lowered my head pretty darn quick.) One of the girls in back began to say, "What are you … " The poor girl. She never finished the question. And she never should have opened her mouth to ask it.

As the pickup met the woodchuck, something more than a splatter occurred. One of the chaperones driving behind me said that it looked as though someone had planted explosives inside the woodchuck. It just blew up. Partially digested alfalfa and its accompanying unpleasant aroma covered my grate, headlights, hood, and windshield. But any carwash can take care of that. The worst damage was done inside the car—and not to the upholstery, either.

We quickly pulled over. My wife and the two girls, chatting carelessly just moments earlier, jumped from the car as if they were on fire. Spitting, plucking, and picking, they desperately tried to get the gunk off themselves. (I stepped out unscathed.) Our two other vehicles stopped, and the kids converged on the scene with roars of laughter. That is, until they got close enough to smell the fallout. A few kids offered the rest of their Cokes to cleanse palates, some T-shirts traded bodies, people pitched in as best they could, and we got ready for the ride home.

It amazed me, and still does years later, that the absolute worst thing that happened on that great canoe trip is the one thing the kids talk about the most. As soon as we reached the church that day, no one told their parents about drifting down the Allegheny. The first report was of how a woodchuck exploded into the pastor's car and took three casualties. And today it is still, "Do you remember when we were driving home from that canoe trip ...?"[15]

Sure, there's nothing in the story of the exploding woodchuck that reveals an obvious (or frontal) catalyst for a deeper commitment to Jesus, but there's plenty in it that makes for a *deeper commitment to a group*—the shared stories of unforgettable events that move people from fringe participation to an owned identity. And once kids identify with the group—its stories become *their stories*—they stay attached long enough to "taste and see" God. It's the sideways experiences contained in exploding woodchuck stories, not necessarily the years spent competing in Bible Bowl, that obliquely lever teenagers into a place where they can make lifelong commitments to Christ. Over the last decade there's been a gathering revolt within the youth ministry community against the kind of silly fun that the exploding woodchuck story represents—critics rightly charge that just-for-fun games and activities are not frontally about the gospel of Jesus. But when they throw fun out with the bathwater, they also lose the leverage they need to open doors that are closed to the gospel. That's why shrewd youth pastors defend this oblique theological equation: Fun x Memorable + Jesus – Boring = Discipleship.

In the world of political activism, those who make a lasting impact have learned, over time, how to approach their great quests more obliquely. Several years ago I watched Ed Bradley interview U2 front man Bono, perhaps the most successful of all the "celebrity activists," on *60 Minutes*. When Bradley asked the Irish rocker how he'd been so successful convincing American leaders to support AIDS research and relief for the African continent, he expected a political/rock star answer but got something far more shrewd instead:

Bradley: Is there a secret to your success—the way you've been able to do this?

Bono: It was probably that it would be really wrong beating a sort of left-wing drum, taking the usual bleeding-heart-liberal line.

Bradley *(voiceover)*: Instead he enlisted the ruling right of American politics.

Bono: Particularly conservative Christians. I was very angry that they were not involved more in the AIDS emergency. I was saying, "This is the leprosy that we read about in the New Testament. You know, Christ hung out with the lepers, but you're ignoring the AIDS emergency. How can you?" And, you know, they said, "Well, you're right, actually. We have been. And we're sorry. We'll get involved." And they did.[16]

Just as Bono's oblique strategy reveals, it's impossible to respond to challenges shrewdly unless you understand how things work. Once you do, you're equipped and ready to bring leverage into the relationship by dancing the tango with those who have what you want. And there's nothing wrong with using oblique methods to get what you want, *as long as what you want is born out of innocence and is driven by God's own agenda.* What God wants is the redemption of His beloved creation, marred by sin—so He uses the oblique method of sacrificing His own Son to get it. He's not at all embarrassed to use force and leverage to redeem us. When my friend Chris Stanton, a longtime missionary to a "closed" Muslim nation and one of the shrewdest people I know, came to visit not long ago, he told me the story of how he convinced the executives of the Muslim nation's national airline to give him free shipping for his medical and educational supplies in perpetuity, a profound grace for someone who has sacrificed so much to care for the poor and disenfranchised in this Muslim country. Chris does not have the natural leverage that a celebrity like Bono brings to the table—he, like most of us, has nothing but his sanctified cunning to use as a lever:

> I went to visit the director of [the Muslim nation's national airline] in New York City. When I introduced myself I told him I love [his country]. And I told him what I have done for [his country]. And I saw his eyes start to glow, and he came around the desk and gave me

a big, warm hug. He said to me: "Anything you want to send to [my country], I will get it there for you." That went on for a few years, and then that guy got transferred. So a new guy came in, and he told me there would be no more free shipping. He was cold as ice. So my gutsy self said, "I'm going to meet with that guy. I'll tell him I'm doing a good work in [his country], and he should support me."

I finagled my appointment—I sent his assistant an email for it, but she didn't get it. So I showed up anyway, and after she told me I had no appointment, I told her I'd take the same time the next day. She gave it to me, and I showed up the next day. I was sent to the board of directors room, waiting for the new head guy. A beautiful young woman came in and sat a few seats from me—it turns out, she was the company lawyer. The president had told her to join him in the meeting. I'm thinking: *Uh-oh, this is a more serious meeting than I thought.* And then the president comes into the room, looking like Steve Jobs. His first words are: "Who do you think you are?" He starts ranting and raving in English about me cutting into his profit margins by taking free cargo from New York. Then he continues his rant in French and Arabic.

Finally he settles down, and I ask him if I can speak. He says yes. I ask for sixty seconds to tell him what I've done for [the people of his country] in the last ten years. And I share about medicines, computers, and humanitarian work. He doesn't seem impressed. And then I open my mouth, and this comes out: "Mr. President, someday you're going to die. When you go to heaven, God is not going to ask you how big your house was or what kind of car you drive. But He might ask you why you didn't allow me to take humanitarian goods to care for your people on [your airline]." He looks at me and says, "Do you have our Ambassador card—our frequent flyer card?" I said, "I have something somewhere with a number on it. But I'm not here to talk about a frequent flyer card, I'm here to talk cargo." And he says, "I'm giving you the cargo. But also with the cargo, I want you to have the card."

That card now gets me into the executive lounge where I get free drinks, the chance to sit in a leather chair, and a lady who walks me through the customs line to the front of the line. I'm treated like a diplomat.[17]

Because Chris has spent years studying how things work with people from this Muslim nation, he's free to dance the tango with the president of the nation's airline, earning through his experiments with an oblique approach what he could never have gained through a more direct complaint or appeal. His appeal to the airline president's love for his people is the sideways leverage that ends up moving the immovable rock. It's this commitment to work indirectly, trusting Jesus in the moment to prompt us to apply the right force in the right place at the right time, that feels like we're dancing the tango. It requires us to study, but it also requires us to trust God and take risks, based on the nuances our Partner gives us. A friend of mine who's a longtime youth pastor asked a small community of peers on Facebook to help her with a problem. Her issue: "The longer I am in youth ministry, the more I'm being criticized by leaders and parents in the church. I really don't like how it feels. How do you all deal with it?" Another youth pastor responded with a shrewd and winsome manifesto: "There are days when I don't think anybody likes me at my church—people can be a pain in the butt sometimes, and it stinks. In September I got complaints for a few weeks in a row. I was thinking about quitting and working at Starbucks. Instead I started dressing professionally on Sundays—not the best way to connect with students, but it worked. Nobody yells at me when I'm dressed up. So put some makeup on, do your hair, and dress up. It sounds silly but it's helped me."[18]

Obliquity is not just a tactic; it's a way of life. And when it is subjugated to the heart and will of God, obliquity delivers the shrewd leverage we need to get things done for a kingdom that is under violent assault. Ultimately, the Parable of the Shrewd Manager is Jesus's most pragmatic teaching—He's highlighting a personal art form that's as functional as a tire iron applied to a hubcap. John Kay writes: "Americans speak a kind of English rather than a kind of French because General James Wolfe captured Quebec in 1759 and made the British Crown the dominant influence in North America. Eschewing more obvious lines of attack, Wolfe's men scaled the precipitous Heights of Abraham and so took the city from the unprepared defenders. The Germans defeated the Maginot Line by going around it. Japanese invaders bicycled through the Malayan jungle to capture Singapore, whose guns face out to sea."[19] Though we're tempted to categorize these great victories as the expected result of progressive strategies, they share more in common with Picasso's "blue period" than they do with the Sudoku puzzle in your local newspaper.

Trusting Daddy

Way back when I had no tinge of gray at my temples, I joined fifty people from eighteen countries at a training school in Rome, Italy— we were there to learn how to be cross-cultural street evangelists. One night in Sicily during an outreach event, a woman came screaming into our midst, apparently possessed by a demon. There was no time to flip through the field manual at that point—and, also, *there is no field manual* for this sort of thing. So I and my other wide-eyed missionary trainees had to trust that God would show us what to do *as we were doing it*. Was she crazy? Was this a prank? If we pray for her, what do we say? What if it doesn't work? These questions, like lightning bolts, flashed and then were gone. So a couple of us decided to open our mouths and see what God would give us to say. We spoke directly (in English, not Italian) to what we supposed was a demon, politely but firmly asking it to leave the woman alone and go away.

Like the skeptic who pulls the trigger and is shocked when the barrel emits a bullet, we were agog when the woman immediately stopped scream-croaking in the scary, guttural way she had been doing. She collapsed on the floor, hyperventilating until the storm passed and she was calm. Apparently, and in spite of ourselves, we used the right force at the right time in the right place to eject that pansy demon from its "squatter" home. In practical terms, moving shrewdly "as we were doing it" meant scaring ourselves to death—in a good way. Like Peter before us, we trusted Jesus enough to get out of our "boat" and walk on water. And like Peter, this decision exposed our faith and diagnosed how much trust had infected and affected our relationship with Jesus. When we dance the tango, trusting Jesus to lead us into oblique and surprising directions, we will discover the intoxicating beauty of the dance. And sometimes we will sink like Peter and scream for Him to rescue us.

Like Emily Wurtzbacher, the competitive ballroom dancer, we're able to dance the tango only because we're relaxed and trusting our Partner to lead us. And, typically, we don't operate in that kind of trust unless we're forced into it by painful circumstance. Pain makes us thirsty for Jesus—desperately dependent and abandoned and (finally) trusting in Someone outside of ourselves. The beauty of desperate dependence is that it makes us thirsty, and thirsty people get to be close to Jesus. In John 7:37 Jesus tells the crowd gathered for the last day of the Feast of Booths: "If anyone is thirsty, let him come to Me and drink." In the awkward silence that followed, maybe the people were chewing on the same question we'd have if we were there:

- Does He have a very large canteen?

Or, alternately, maybe they were asking more serious questions about the vaguely appealing offer Jesus put on the table:

- Do I know if my soul is thirsty?
- If I'm thirsty, what am I thirsty for?

- Can Jesus quench my thirst?
- What sort of water is He offering me?

If you think about the interactions Jesus had—the stories He told, and the life He lived—desperation played a role in most of them. It's a central force in all of His relationships, and it's also the theme of His most famous story, the parable of the prodigal son. Desperation is our basic thirst, and it's the mind-set God prefers in us. The psalmist knows what this feels like: "As the deer pants for the water brooks, so my soul pants for You, O God. My soul thirsts for God, for the living God" (Ps. 42:1–2). Desperation is also a central element in nearly every good film, because we're drawn to people facing desperation—this is one big reason *It's a Wonderful Life* has such enduring power, year after year. We're fascinated by how people like George Bailey respond to their own desperation, and we can't help but live vicariously through them. We were created to trust God more wholly than Emily Wurtzbacher trusts her daddy. But so many of us, as Emily's tango partner observed, have a shattered trust with our "Daddy-God." We can trace the break back to Genesis 3:1–5:

> Now the serpent was more crafty than any of the
> wild animals the LORD God had made. He said to
> the woman, "Did God really say, 'You must not eat
> from any tree in the garden'?"
>
> The woman said to the serpent, "We may eat fruit
> from the trees in the garden, but God did say, 'You must
> not eat fruit from the tree that is in the middle of the
> garden, and you must not touch it, or you will die.'"

"You will not surely die," the serpent said to the
woman. "For God knows that when you eat of it
your eyes will be opened, and you will be like God,
knowing good and evil." (NIV)

We all know what happens next. Eve eats the fruit and then
gives it to Adam to eat. Because of what Satan told her—or dangled
in front of her—she's drawn to the forbidden fruit. What's powerful
enough to convince her to betray the God she's always trusted? Satan
promises she can become like God—self-sufficient and in charge of
her own destiny. Adam quickly follows her lead. Together, they put
their faith in the false hope that they can be gods. But in the kingdom of God, if you believe you're a god, you cast yourself outside of
relationship with the one true God. We're literally sick with the myth
of our own self-sufficiency. Desperation serves as a medicine that
helps make us well. When self-sufficiency fails us, desperation leads
us back to a trusting relationship with God. Desperation reminds us
that we're not God—we never have been, we're not right now, and
we never will be. It tells us we're not in control. It opens the door for
us to trust Him again, and that's what fuels our oblique approaches
to the challenges and opportunities we face in life.

People who are not desperate are also not thirsty—they won't
move beyond their false belief of their own god-ness, and therefore
live in bondage to the lie-leech that's sucking all the trust out of their
relationship with God. When we feel in control and self-sufficient we
say to ourselves, whether or not we'll admit it, that we really don't need
God. More bluntly, Oswald Chambers says: "The more you fulfill
yourself the less you will seek God."[20] But, deep down, doubt about

our claims of self-sufficiency nag at us. Desperation is an open door to the truth, to true freedom: "I am not God, I've never been God, I don't want to be God. I am simply a branch that will die apart from the Vine, who is Jesus" (John 15:5, author paraphrase). During Jesus's ministry on earth, the people who seemed to "get" this also got to hang out with Him (the woman who touched the hem of Jesus's garment, the prostitute at the party of Pharisees, Zaccheus the tax collector, that Canaanite woman whom Jesus called a "dog," and many more). Jesus preferred hanging out with desperate people. They were His closest friends—He was drawn to their desperate hearts like a magnet. Why?

Well, *all of us* prefer to hang out with people who see us well— people who are truthful and loving mirrors of who we are, people who *enjoy us* for who we really are. That's what makes trusting intimacy possible. And desperate people see Jesus well. They know they're *not* God. They know that Jesus *is* God. They sense that He's the source of their life and that they need Him to take the lead in their own version of the tango. They base their relationship with Him on the truth of their "taste" of Him. This beckons them into an intimate relationship with Him and gradually restores their trust. Chambers, author of *My Utmost for His Highest,* set out to explore the crucial role of desperation in our relationship with Jesus when he wrote "Receiving Yourself in the Fires of Sorrow," prefacing his meditation with Jesus's own exclamation of desperation in John 12:27–28: "What shall I say, 'Father, save Me from this hour'? But for this purpose I came to this hour. 'Father, glorify Your name.'"

> We say that there ought to be no sorrow, but there *is*
> sorrow, and we have to accept and receive ourselves in

its fires. If we try to evade sorrow, refusing to deal with
it, we are foolish. Sorrow is one of the biggest facts in
life, and there is no use in saying it should not be. Sin,
sorrow, and suffering *are*, and it is not for us to say that
God has made a mistake in allowing them....

You cannot find or receive yourself through success, because you lose your head over pride.... And
you cannot receive yourself through the monotony
of your daily life, because you give in to complaining. The only way to find yourself is in the fires of
sorrow. Why it should be this way is immaterial. The
fact is that it is true in the Scriptures and in human
experience. You can always recognize who has been
through the fires of sorrow and received himself, and
you know that you can go to him in your moment
of trouble and find that he has plenty of time for
you. But if a person has not been through the fires
of sorrow, he is apt to be contemptuous, having no
respect or time for you, only turning you away. If
you will receive yourself in the fires of sorrow, God
will make you nourishment for other people.[21]

In 2002 fourteen-year-old William Kamkwamba's country of
Malawi was suffering through one of the worst droughts in its history,
and desperation drove William to follow the sort of quixotic dream you
only read about in adventure stories. With his family and others surviv-
ing on one meal a day, William set himself to understand how things
work in the midst of a catastrophe that had turned the red-soil farmland

into a parched and forbidding wasteland. William and his people were experiencing terrible shortages of everything except one natural resource: wind. "I wanted to do something to help and change things," William said in an interview with CNN.com writer Faith Karimi. "Then I said to myself, 'If they can make electricity out of wind, I can try, too.'"[22]

After school officials kicked William out because he could not pay eighty dollars in back fees, he had plenty of time on his hands to figure out a shrewd, oblique response to a natural disaster. Motivated by his own "fires of sorrow," he went to his old school's lending library and borrowed *Using Energy*, an eighth-grade American textbook with a cover photo that showed a long row of towering windmills, which "appeared so powerful that they made the photo itself appear to be in motion."[23] After poring over the book, William taught himself to build a windmill. He first built a prototype using a radio motor. Then he collected junkyard scraps and built a working tower with five-meter blades out of bicycle parts, plastic pipes, tractor fan blades, an old shock absorber, and car batteries.[24] This Rube Goldberg contraption managed to power four light bulbs and charge his neighbors' mobile phones.[25] Out of this early success, William managed to build five windmills, including one that's thirty-seven feet tall. Though he was mocked like his ancestor Noah was many millenniums ago—his neighbors in the tiny village of Masitala called him "misala," the Malawian word for "crazy"—the gangly contraptions he built now generate electricity and pump water in his hometown near the Malawi capital of Lilongwe.[26]

With the help of donors, William, now twenty-three, studies at the elite African Leadership Academy. Al Gore, the former US vice president, has used William's work as an example of green ingenuity.

And business leaders regularly invite him to regale groups of entre-preneurs with his oblique approach to drought relief—"the people of this world are more shrewd in dealing with their own kind than are the people of the light." In the end, a fourteen-year-old boy grew desperate enough to study how things work, then take a costly step of faith and trust to bring his dream to reality, becoming a source of "nourishment for other people," just as Oswald Chambers describes. One boy who "received himself in the fires of sorrow," daring to dance the tango, did something shrewd to bring life to his village.

We don't *have* to be in pain to feel desperate for Jesus, but pain's pedigree as a catalyst for desperation is unassailable. It is also unde-niably possible—through our often-slow journey from a "distant uncle" relationship with Jesus to a "Master and Lover" relationship with Him—to simply *choose* a thirsty, desperate relationship with Him. This will lead us, as Paul advises, to fall on the stone of stum-bling before it (or He) falls on us.

> *What's that on the ground?*
> *It's what's left of my heart*
> *Somebody named Jesus*
> *Broke it to pieces*
> *And planted the shards*
> *And they're coming up green*
> *And they're coming in bloom*
> *I can hardly believe*
> *This is all coming true*

—Andrew Peterson, "Just As I Am"[27]

Chapter 4

The Way of Gamaliel & The Great Knock

*In any deal, you need to know your opponent's break-
ing point. To assess that, you might call them late
at night or at the weekend. If they take the call,
you know they're desperate. And from that moment
on, you know you have the upper hand.*
—"Swifty" Lazar, agent for former President
Richard Nixon, advising Nixon on how he intends
to get a big-money deal from talk-show host
David Frost for a series of historic interviews, in
the film *Frost/Nixon*

*God has a way of giving by the cartloads to
those who give away by shovelfuls.*
—C. H. Spurgeon

*You thought you were going to be made into a decent
little cottage: but He is building a palace.*
—C. S. Lewis, *Mere Christianity*

There once was a foul, hateful man named Saul who was knocked off his horse by God, temporarily blinded, renamed Paul, then set loose to play a primary role in establishing the church of Jesus Christ around the world. I'm pretty sure that's *not* how most people are invited into relationship with Jesus. My story? When I was ten I responded to an altar call at the end of a Pat Boone concert—slightly less epic, and 100 percent more embarrassing. In contrast, the story of Saul's "conversion" is oddly menacing—like an episode from *The Sopranos*. It's not God's habit to go around assaulting people, maiming them, then sliding "an offer they can't refuse" across the table while they're desperately worried if they'll ever see daylight again. In a Christian culture that is over-served with how-to books, *nobody's* writing books about "Maim 'Em and Claim 'Em" evangelism. We like to say that God is a gentleman; He invites but never forces. And that's true in almost every instance, except for the glaring exception of His strong-arm job with Saul. So the elephant-question in the living room is simply, *Why?*

Well, what if you had a job that was so specialized that your pool of qualified candidates was … *severely limited*? Like, for instance, "Helicopter Lineman for Live Transmission Wires"—a real-life candidate for the World's Most Dangerous Job. When the job is hyper-specialized, no cattle-call recruiting effort will work—you'll have to go after your preferred pick personally. Let's say you find all the characteristics you're looking for in one man, so you study this man to understand how he works. Then you apply the right force at the right time in the right place to land him. In this case, your "right force" will have to overcome the slight hurdle of the candidate's utter hatred for you. What to do? I can hear Tony Soprano cracking his knuckles....

Of course, Paul has the freedom to reject "the offer he can't refuse," just like all of us. God is rolling the dice on him, counting on something He sees in Paul's heart that lurks underneath all his blustering self-righteousness. Imagine what was listed on the job description that God handed to Paul, the once-and-always "Pharisee of Pharisees," after the blinded and hobbled and broken man signed on the dotted line:

Job Title: Combat Church Planter **Job Code:** 777

Department: Mergers & Acquisitions **Job Grade:** Martyr

Position Overview

Plant and propagate the church of Jesus Christ throughout the known ancient world, without regard for personal safety, comfort, or future career considerations.

Essential Job Functions

• Preach to the Gentiles the unfathomable riches of Christ.

• Bring to light what is the "administration of the mystery which for ages has been hidden in God who created all things."

• Make known the manifold wisdom of God to the rulers and the authorities in the heavenly places.

• Bow before the Father so that He will grant that Christ may dwell in the hearts of all those you come in contact with, through faith.

(Ephesians 3:14, 17)

• Help all those you come in contact with to comprehend with all the saints what is the breadth and length and height and depth of the love of Christ, which surpasses knowledge, that they may be filled up to all the fullness of God.

(Ephesians 3:8–19)

Non-Essential Job Functions

• All things are lawful, but employee will consider that not all things are profitable.

• All things are lawful, but employee will refuse to be mastered by anything.

(1 Corinthians 6:12)

Requirements

• Living as a man "condemned to death"—becoming a "spectacle to the world, both to angels and to men."

• Acting as a "fool for Christ's sake"—weak when others are strong and without honor when others are distinguished.

• Able to endure hunger, thirst, and poor clothing—with an expectation of "rough treatment" and homelessness.

• Able to toil, "working with your own hands."

• When reviled, able to bless; when persecuted, able to endure; when slandered, able to conciliate.

• Willingness to embrace status as "scum of the world, the dregs of all things."

(1 Corinthians 4:9–13)

Salary

Position currently has no salary. Compensation is in the form of "the surpassing value of knowing Christ Jesus your Lord" (Phil. 3:8). Employee will need to work a second job to support this prestigious opportunity.

NOTE: This job description is not intended to be all-inclusive. Employee may perform other related duties as negotiated to meet the ongoing needs of the organization.

So God needs someone who can travel the known world, planting churches and pastoring new converts while he's perpetually hunted like quarry—always on the move, never leaving the perils of his own personal lion's den. This person will need to cover great distances with few allies through challenging, uncharted, and often dangerous country, into and out of cultures that are vastly different from his own. He will need to be smart and perseverant and passionate and … naturally shrewd. If you've ever wondered why God would choose Saul of Tarsus, a bald-faced, cold-hearted, murderous enemy—*an Old Man Potter*—to lead His worldwide invasion force, my manufactured job description offers a few clues. In 1 Timothy 1:13, Paul admits that "I was once a blasphemer and a persecutor and a violent man" (NIV). And that's just the ticket. Simply, Jesus needed the shrewdest man He could find for this mission, whether or not that man believed in Him or loved Him or followed Him—minor details, really, that were quickly overcome by a little misery and fear. He needed a man who was well acquainted with the use of force in his relationships ("a persecutor and a violent man"), because that force could be redirected from evil pursuits to innocent crusades.

Jesus found his man in Saul, later Paul, who described himself this way in his defense before a hostile mob in Jerusalem that was bent on killing him:

> I am a Jew, born in Tarsus of Cilicia, but brought up
> in this city, educated under Gamaliel, strictly accord-
> ing to the law of our fathers, being zealous for God
> just as you all are today. I persecuted this Way to the
> death, binding and putting both men and women
> into prisons, as also the high priest and all the Council
> of the elders can testify. From them I also received
> letters to the brethren, and started off for Damascus in
> order to bring even those who were there to Jerusalem
> as prisoners to be punished. (Acts 22:3–6)

This is an Old Man Potter description—a violent (forceful) man well used to using his inborn and educated shrewdness to "kill, steal, and destroy." Under the influence of shrewd he plotted and strategized against the people of God, just as "his father the devil" had done for so long. But Jesus, the Sensei of Shrewd, saw a "man after His own heart"—all that remained was to redeem Saul's cunning and link that "transmission" to the "engine" of Jesus's redemptive purposes instead. This also explains why God changed Saul's name to Paul—an outward symbol of an inner transformation. And while this transformation was singular and personal to Paul, it was also plural and widespread, eventually changing the world. The qualities

God was after were potent and rare—the result of the "cerebral upgrade" Paul had already received from one of the giants of the ancient Hebrew world. Paul, it turns out, was among the elite students tutored by Gamaliel the Elder, perhaps the greatest rabbi in the long history of the Jews.

Earning an MSL Degree

Gamaliel, a Pharisee and the most respected leader in the Sanhedrin, mentored more than five hundred rabbinical students over the course of his life. According to the historians Josephus and Philo, there were likely only six thousand or so Pharisees in the whole world at the time, so that places Gamaliel as the leader of the most prestigious and influential school of Pharisaic Judaism in the ancient world. After his death around AD 50, a Sanhedrin historian wrote: "Since Rabban Gamaliel the Elder died, there has been no more reverence for the law, and purity and piety died out at the same time."[1] Clearly, few Hebrew religious leaders were better known and more respected than Gamaliel.

Saul of Tarsus came from a family of privilege whose patriarch was also a Pharisee—his father was essentially an aristocrat. And just as many privileged patriarchs before and since have done, the father sent the son to the best boarding school in "the old country." In *Not a Fan*, author Kyle Idleman describes the complicated and demanding process that faced a budding rabbi like Paul: "For those students wanting to become the Talmid [or 'disciple'] of a particular rabbi, there was an application process. There were hefty pre-requisites before even being considered. These were the equivalent of the GPA and transcript pre-requisites for getting into an elite college or academy. If you want to go to Harvard, you better have a 4.0 GPA, or a 36 on your ACT, or a 2400 SAT score. Without those kinds of stats, you're probably not going to cut it. The same goes for a Talmid applying to join a rabbi's school."[2] And Gamaliel's school was the cream of the crop.

From the sketchy descriptions we have of Saul's relationship with Gamaliel, it's likely this whip-smart boy was also a hell-raiser. The Talmud implies this description when it highlights a Gamaliel student who was known for his "impudence in learning"—scholars often identify the unnamed student as Saul of Tarsus. In any case, the young Saul quickly distinguishes himself as a budding academic star. The top leaders in Jerusalem appoint him to eradicate the cancerous growth of Christianity in Damascus, and he is personally connected to King Agrippa, his sister Bernice, and Felix, the governor of Jerusalem.

In the New Testament, Gamaliel surfaces most prominently after the apostles are imprisoned in Jerusalem because they refuse to stop preaching about Jesus in the temple's public square. The high priest demands to know why Peter and his companions have ignored the Council's "strict orders not to continue teaching in this name" (Acts 5:28) and Peter infuriates the whole Senate with his impertinent response:

> We must obey God rather than men. The God of
> our fathers raised up Jesus, whom you had put to
> death by hanging Him on a cross. He is the one
> whom God exalted to His right hand as a Prince
> and a Savior, to grant repentance to Israel, and

forgiveness of sins. And we are witnesses of these
things; and so is the Holy Spirit, whom God has
given to those who obey Him. (vv. 29–32)

The offense of this response was so great that the Senate quickly
huddles to decide the most expeditious way to execute the men. They
have already proven, with Jesus, that they are skilled at that sort of
occupation. Into that volatile feeding frenzy the voice of a shrewd
man, Paul's old tutor, booms:

Men of Israel, take care what you propose to do
with these men. For some time ago Theudas rose up,
claiming to be somebody, and a group of about four
hundred men joined up with him. But he was killed,
and all who followed him were dispersed and came
to nothing. After this man, Judas of Galilee rose
up in the days of the census and drew away some
people after him; he too perished, and all those who
followed him were scattered. (vv. 35–37)

To this point, Gamaliel's counsel serves only to fuel the murderous
impulses of his colleagues—now they are *really* worked up. But the
first part of his discourse is like chum in the water for circling sharks.
He draws them close in, winning them over, and then spears them
with this: "So in the present case, I say to you, stay away from these
men and let them alone, for if this plan or action is of men, it will be
overthrown; but if it is of God, you will not be able to overthrow them;
or else you may even be found fighting against God" (vv. 38–39).

This response, like Jesus's shrewd response to the lynch mob that threatens to stone to death a woman caught in adultery (John 8), quickly and radically defuses an explosive situation. The rabbi's oblique solution to this nuclear meltdown is so surprising and inventive that physicists now use "Gamaliel's Principle" to explain a basic assumption in thermodynamics: "The long-term course of future events—consequent to a particular antecedent event—is strictly correlated with the truth quality of the antecedent event."[3] In layman's terms, this means that the long-term future consequence of anything labeled as truth is directly tied to its previous truthfulness.

And the namesake of Gamaliel's Principle, one of the cleverest men in history, is the man Paul lived with and learned from, growing up in the world's best graduate school for shrewd, where he earned his MSL (Master's in Shrewd Living). Of the few snatches of teaching attributed to Gamaliel that remain intact through history, his best known is a quartet of metaphoric comparisons he uses to quickly classify his students, all of them types of fish that are archetypes:

1. A Ritually Impure Fish—one who has memorized everything by studying but has no understanding and is the son of poor parents.
2. A Ritually Pure Fish—one who has learned and understood everything and is the son of rich parents.
3. A Fish from the Jordan River—one who has learned everything but doesn't know how to respond.
4. A Fish from the Mediterranean Sea—one who has learned everything and knows how to respond.[4]

In Gamaliel's shorthand, Paul is a passionate, committed, and fervent "Fish #4." The bulk of the New Testament, and particularly the book of Romans, offers ample evidence of a man "who has learned everything, and knows how to respond"—a clear echo of "understanding how things work, then leveraging that knowledge toward a favored outcome." Paul's letters to the early church read like a series of master's thesis papers written to earn an MSL.

In the first seven chapters of Paul's letter to the Romans he, like his master Gamaliel, throws chum in the water. Here, he artfully paints a picture of our utter inability to overcome sin and the death that it produces in us, ending with a raw plea that is magnetic in its universality: "Wretched man that I am! Who will set me free from the body of this death?" (7:24). If we are tracking with Paul, we are wretched with him—his argument has the force of a swelling torrent. If he leaves us hanging here, suicide becomes a rational response to our reality. But he, channeling his beloved Rabbi Gamaliel, then *spears us* with the hope of our redemption:

> Thanks be to God through Jesus Christ our Lord! …
> There is now no condemnation for those who are in
> Christ Jesus. For the law of the Spirit of life in Christ
> Jesus has set you free from the law of sin and of death.
> For what the Law could not do, weak as it was through
> the flesh, God did: sending His own Son in the likeness
> of sinful flesh and as an offering for sin, He condemned
> sin in the flesh, so that the requirement of the Law
> might be fulfilled in us, who do not walk according to
> the flesh but according to the Spirit. (7:25–8:4)

Paul is at his apologetically shrewdest in his letter to the Christians living in Rome. The first half of the letter lowers every defense we try to mount against the onslaught of redemption; the second half of the letter rescues us from the cliff's edge of obliterated hope. In Martin Luther's *Preface to the Letter of St. Paul to the Romans*, he writes what theologians and Christian leaders from across the denominational spectrum and throughout history have wholeheartedly asserted:

> This epistle is truly the chief part of the New Testament, and is truly the purest gospel. It is worthy not only that every Christian should know it word for word, by heart, but also that he should occupy himself with it every day, as the daily bread of the soul. We can never read it or ponder over it too much; for the more we deal with it, the more precious it becomes and the better it tastes.[5]

And this is why, as I wrote in the introduction to this book: "[Shrewd people] bring life and light and freedom to those around them. Sometimes, they change the world." Fueled by Old Man Potter shrewdness, washed in innocence, the apostle Paul …

- leveraged his extensive knowledge of the Law and the Torah to repeatedly prove to the Jews what seemed far-fetched to them—that Jesus was the promised Messiah (Acts 13:16–41).
- laid the groundwork for a massive expansion of the early church by using Old Testament prophecy to

crack open the gospel's door to the Gentiles (vv. 46–47).

- redirected his "all-in" personality—his naturally zealous makeup—to exercise the kind of faith that habitually "sets the captives free"—bringing healing and deliverance to so many, in such over-the-top circumstances, that the astonished crowds ascribed divinity to him: "The gods have become like men and have come down to us" (Acts 14:8–18).

- became the go-to emissary to a host of fledgling church plants around the ancient world, deputized by the Jerusalem apostles to encourage and correct and admonish new believers who were, most often, trying to figure out how to follow Jesus in isolation from the wider body (Acts 15).

- converted his own suicidal jailer to Christ by staying in his cell even after a God-induced earthquake shook open the doors: "Do not harm yourself, for we are all here!" (Acts 16:22–34).

- exercised his world-class education to engage and upend the leading thinkers and influencers of his day, even out-debating the heavyweight Greeks on Mars Hill (Acts 17:22–31).

- became the first to baptize new believers in the Holy Spirit, resulting in the wholesale release of the gifts of the Spirit, including prophecy (Acts 19:1–6).

- had such a strong "smell" of Jesus on him that people rubbed their handkerchiefs and aprons on

him, then laid those pieces of fabric on their sick
family members and friends to heal them (Acts
19:11–12). Later, he embraced a dead man who'd
fallen from a third-story window ledge and brought
him back to life (Acts 20:7–12).

- shrewdly divided those opposed to him and were
intent on killing him by proclaiming before a
council of Pharisees and Sadducees: "'I am a
Pharisee, a son of Pharisees; I am on trial for the
hope and resurrection of the dead!' As he said this,
there occurred a dissension between the Pharisees
and Sadducees, and the assembly was divided. For
the Sadducees say that there is no resurrection,
nor an angel, nor a spirit, but the Pharisees
acknowledge them all" (Acts 23:6–8).

Paul's remarkable story confirms that nothing has the leverage
to open us and redeem us more profoundly than an "innocent as
a dove" person behaving as "shrewd as a serpent." Far from their
negative reputation, shrewd thinking and shrewd behavior have laid
the foundation for most of the things we consider treasures in life,
including the undisputed champion of twentieth-century apologists,
C. S. Lewis. Lewis's story is remarkably like Paul's story—both began
their arc in complete opposition to God and His kingdom but later
became the leading apologists of their time. Both were highly educated "star" students whose vigorous intellects and relentless passion
allowed the gospel to penetrate deep into hostile territory. Both had
a practiced ability to influence massive numbers of people through

their speaking and writing. And both had natural gifts of shrewd-ness that were honed razor-sharp under the tutelage of a master who remained staunchly outside the Christian community.

In the Beginning There Was "The Great Knock"

It's hard to overestimate the forming influence wielded by William T. Kirkpatrick—a determined atheist, former headmaster of Lurgan College in Northern Ireland, and longtime family friend of Albert and Flora Lewis. Because young "Jack" Lewis grew up in a home with a father profoundly distracted by the grief of his wife's death and a brother who was mostly away at boarding school, he later filled the father-void in his life by closely attaching himself to the man he nicknamed "The Great Knock." For three years, starting in 1914, Lewis lived in the Kirkpatrick home. Mrs. Kirkpatrick fed him home-cooked meals, and Mr. Kirkpatrick fed him a steady diet of the classics in Greek, Latin, and Italian literature. Lewis historian Lyle Dorsett writes:

> Kirkpatrick not only pushed the teenaged Ulster lad
> to read great literature in the original languages, he
> taught him to think critically and analytically as well
> as how to express himself logically and clearly....
> [However] "The Great Knock" taught C. S. Lewis
> more than how to think and read intelligently. An
> atheist, rationalist, and pessimist, the retired school-
> master reinforced his pupil's already well-formed
> disdain for people who could believe in the existence

and goodness of God without palpable evidence. Truth, as C. S. Lewis learned, is eminently worth pursuing. But the teaching he received insisted that the pathway to truth came only through reason.

Kirkpatrick's teachings left permanent marks on C. S. Lewis. The writer's clear language, careful thoughts, meticulous logic, and persuasive evidence reflect the old teacher's care in developing a brilliant young mind.[6]

In *Surprised by Joy*, Lewis's riveting memoir of his path from atheist to Christian apologist, first published in 1955, the Oxford don describes The Great Knock's relentless commitment to teaching his pupil the foundations of shrewd—to understand how things work, then leverage that knowledge to move people from point A to point C:

> The idea that human beings should exercise their vocal organs for any purpose except that of communicating or discovering truth was to him preposterous. The most casual remark was taken as a summons to disputation. I soon came to know the differing values of his three openings. The loud cry of "Stop!" was flung in to arrest a torrent of verbiage which could not be endured for a moment longer; not because it fretted his patience (he never thought of that) but because it was wasting time, darkening counsel. The hastier and quieter "Excuse!" (*i.e.,* "Excuse me") ushered in a correction or distinction merely parenthetical and

betokened that, thus set right, your remark might still,

without absurdity, be allowed to reach completion.

The most encouraging of all was, "I hear you." This

meant that your remark was significant and only

required refutation; it had risen to the dignity of error.[7]

The Great Knock taught Lewis the rhythms of debate as if he was teaching him to fence—the parry-and-thrust probing of an opponent's position, then the precise offensive stabs at unguarded openings until the point of the sword skewers the heart of the argument. Bowling Green professor of English Bruce Edwards defines Kirkpatrick's style of aggressive and leveraging wordplay as an "exaggerated version of Socratic dialogue."[8]

Named after the classical Greek philosopher Socrates, Socratic dialogue is a question-based dialectical method (two opposing views considered together) designed to win an argument by subverting your opponent's position—the goal is to shrewdly lure your enemy into contradicting himself. It's a "negative method of hypothesis elimination," a kind of *Survivor* competition in which inferior explanations are systematically "voted off the island." "Negative method" is really just another way of describing "oblique"—people who are adept at Socratic dialogue win arguments systematically, but *sideways*. When it works well, the opponent never sees the dagger coming. The idea is to gradually lever your opponent into agreeing with the premise of your argument by asking a series of questions, then "parrying" with your surprise conclusion. For example, what if your goal was to prove the ontological existence of God? First, you maneuver your opponent into agreeing with this premise: "If God exists, then wouldn't He be the greatest of all conceivable beings?" Even atheists would assent to this statement, even though they passionately disagree with the truth of it.

The Socratic artist then asks this question: "Is a being that exists greater than one that does not exist?" The question itself is framed in a way that's hard to resist, setting the opponent up for this coup de grâce: "Therefore God must exist—if He didn't, He would not be the greatest conceivable being (and therefore would not qualify as God)."

Socratic dialogue is akin to the most effective strategy modern chess champions use, pioneered by the legendary William Steinitz, the nineteenth-century chess master and the most dominant player in history. Although he first won renown for his frontal "attacking" style, in 1873 he dumped that approach for a shrewder strategy he called "positional play." In it, players dominate by maneuvering their pieces for long-term leverage, rather than short-term attacks and threats. This strategy "require[es] judgment more than extensive calculation of variations."[9] It's dancing the tango instead of the waltz.

Though the atheist beliefs of The Great Knock at first led Lewis farther away from the nominal faith he'd embraced as a young boy, before his mother died and bitter resentment drove him from God, his training circle of shrewd thinking formed the foundation for Lewis's fame as the contemporary world's most fearsome defender of faith in Christ. In this way Lewis and the apostle Paul are "twin brothers of different mothers"—both of them formed by the razor intellect of a master of shrewd, both of them using their skills to apply the right force in the right place at the right time to build corridors of light in a wasteland of darkness.

Chapter 5

The Shadow of the Snake

The most potent weapon in the hands of the oppressor is the mind of the oppressed.
—Steven Biko, *I Write What I Like*

A vigorous temper is not altogether an evil. Men who are easy as an old shoe are generally of little worth.
—C. H. Spurgeon, *Lectures to My Students*

Your whole life is on your shoulders when you're playing pool. I can tell if you're disciplined or undisciplined. Some of the girls have real poker faces. You can't tell if they're upset. But if you show me any emotion while playing the game, well, that's why they call me The Viper. If I sense any weakness, well, it's all over.
—Melissa Little, the top female billiards player in the US

Old Aesop's fable: You are known by the company you keep. New Sweet's fable: You can tell a Christian by the enemies he/she makes.
—Leonard Sweet

For thousands of years Satan has been reading one book, and that book is the heart of man.
—James Ryle

It's early in the morning, and I'm standing in line with Lucy at McDonald's—we're grabbing something quick to eat before I drop her off at middle school for a student council meeting. Directly in front of us in line is an elderly man—not unusual because, as you may know, elderly people are the primary clientele of McDonald's before 7:00 a.m. It is finally the man's turn to order, so he lays down the newspaper he's been reading in line and steps forward. Fixing his predator stare on the young immigrant woman behind the counter, he barks his order. The sound of his voice is jarring, like he's firing an automatic weapon: "Coffee. Biscuit. Strawberry jam." She struggles to process his rapid-fire order, just as I do. He repeats himself, now sounding like a jackhammer. And then, with fear in her eyes and in her movements, she scurries to get his order. She turns and holds up a packet of grape jelly: "Did you want *grape* jelly?" And he, cold as a blade, stares at her and snarls: "What did I say before?" She looks at him, pleading for mercy. And he says, only: "Well?" And she responds with one of the most courageous questions I've ever heard: "Was it strawberry?" Like a viper, he hisses: "*That's what I said.*" And now she's unsure of everything. She holds up his biscuit and asks, "Was there anything else?" And he blasts away again: "Coffee. Biscuit.

Strawberry jam." All of this happens in a few seconds, much faster than it has taken you to read my slow-motion version of it. And at this point I can't restrain myself from responding to his assault—I have to intervene: "Sir," I tell the man in a firm voice, "you are treating her with brutality." Ignoring me, he grabs his tray and his paper and shuffles off to join the other elderly men nattering away in their glassed-in cage—not wholly unlike a guard at Auschwitz heading to the mess hall after his shift at the gas chamber.

The effect of this short interchange is like lighting the fuse to my testosterone—the brutalized counter girl must be avenged. And the form of my vengeance, I decide, will be to offer her my direct eye contact, followed by, "I'm so sorry. You have a lot of courage." But brutalized people feel the shame of it, and it is hard for this girl to receive my apology or my encouragement. So I smile, as tenderly as I know how to do, and thank her for her service to us. Mr. Auschwitz is eating his biscuit and talking baseball with his buddies when Lucy and I walk through the door, headed to our car. My daughter, typical of a middle schooler who is sure the whole world is watching and judging her every move, is embarrassed that I created a minor scene at the counter when I confronted the man. I am lost in thought, thinking about how Mr. Auschwitz knew exactly how to apply the right force at the right time in the right place to get what he wanted—and how evil the whole thing was. His intention (I'm guessing it was because she was an immigrant) was to make this girl *feel the way he saw her*—like an insignificant piece of trash. This menacing man used the leverage of shrewd to "kill, steal, and destroy," and my morning was now infected with the stench of death, also known as the cologne of Satan.

Shrewd, we remember, is neutral—just as a nail gun can be used to build a beautiful home or, as the Russian Mafia knows, execute a rival gang member. Or just as a wrench can be used to fix an engine or, as any reader of Agatha Christie knows, as a bludgeon in the hand of a guilty butler. Or just as a chain saw can be used to cut down dead trees or, in the case of *The Texas Chainsaw Massacre*, for somewhat bloodier purposes. Satan has taken something created and practiced by God and used it, so often, to crush the hopes of immigrant counter-girls. And this is why we're generally repelled by shrewdness.

Both Jesus and Satan wield the wrench of shrewd in all things, at all times—Jesus uses it to fix us; Satan uses it to *fix* us. We're far more familiar with the nasty, menacing, conniving ways evil people use shrewdness to *harm us* than we are with the kind, artful, and redemptive ways God uses shrewdness to *free us*. My friend Joe Marinich, a pastor, once confessed to me: "I always tell my wife that I would love to be on *Survivor*, but I'd never try to do it. I understand the game, and I would want to play it the way it's supposed to be played. However, as a pastor, I am afraid that by being shrewd in the game I would make pastors look bad. To win *Survivor* you need to be shrewd, yet those who *are* shrewd are always seen as the villains. Boston Rob, Russell, and the other villains were all great at watching, observing, and adjusting—yet people hate them."[1]

If you think about the Parable of the Shrewd Manager in the context of *Survivor*, the shiftless-but-shrewd antihero of the story would fit nicely into the shoes of the show's infamous bad guys—all of them have few redeeming qualities apart from their masterful ability to apply the right force at the right time in the right place. And so, when Jesus constructs a story that highlights His admiration for the Boston

Robs of the world, we're left scrambling to understand how evil can be good. This is why, when Jesus tells the disciples (a group that includes you and me) that they must be "as shrewd as serpents and as innocent as doves," He uses a rhetorical trick called a "merism" to combine two mutually exclusive concepts into one intertwined truth. Simply, a merism conveys the deeper essence of something by using multiple and contrasting parts to describe one thought. For example, "lock, stock, and barrel" is a merism that describes the totality of something by referencing contrasting parts of a gun. Or in Genesis 1:1, when God creates "the heavens and the earth," we know the writer means to pound home the point that God created everything, and he uses a merism to do it. Or, in Psalm 139, King David uses a merism to reflect back to God that he's known by Him at his core: "You know when I sit down and when I rise up" (v. 2). So, with "shrewd as serpents" and "innocent as doves," Jesus uses two contrasting metaphors to help us wholly understand the way He wants us to live. And we must live "as shrewd as serpents and as innocent as doves" because, bluntly, our Enemy is the mother of all terrorists.

The cultural climate that is our reality—one that not only is grimly described in the Bible as "the world forces of this darkness" (Eph. 6:12) but is obvious to anyone who is not sheltered by suburban bubble wrap—is oppositional and profane and dismissive and patrolled by the terrorist insurgents of Lucifer, and we often seem shocked and offended by it as Christians. It's the same way we'd be shocked if our neighbor, in broad daylight, spray-painted a threatening obscenity on our garage door. "How dare you defile my home!" But, of course, the world is not our "home"—for many people, it seems more like a gulag. And Jesus made sure to remind all His followers that if the world hated Him, it would certainly hate them. Our functional response to that warning is a wink and a smile. But when we see clear evidence that the world—and, again, by "world" I mean the "rulers," the "powers," and "the spiritual forces of wickedness in the heavenly places"—really *does* hate us, we're surprised, offended, and indignant. The "Ruler of this world" is, indeed, a terrorist. He knows that most of us are ill prepared to deal with his shrewd brutality—just as the immigrant counter-girl was helpless in the face of Mr. Auschwitz's improvised explosive devices. Terrorists know that those who are willing to kill always have leverage over those who have vowed *never* to kill.

Dancing with the Adversary

I was sitting in a booth at Panera Bread, restless and anxious and dreading the conversation I was about to have with my friend Bob Krulish (the director of the pastoral staff at my church). I could feel the specter of my humiliation creeping around the corner. The short version of my travail: for months I'd been locked in what felt like a fight to the death with my own Mr. Auschwitz, a man intent on destroying one of my ministry dreams. He'd already found a way to undermine and ultimately kill a ministry outreach that was on the cusp of success after years of hard work and investment. I never saw the flash from the barrel of his gun. And that's because this guy was shrewd, and I wasn't—the truth of this had only lately dawned on me, because I had no idea that shrewdly evil people often hide out in the church, where they can leverage the margins that grace and niceness offer them. And now, as he had baby #2 in his crosshairs, I felt hopeless, alone, and ashamed of my inability to stop the inevitable. In short, I was grappling with the reality that I was too confused and ignorant and direct and … *unsuspecting* … to stop a shrewd predator from destroying something I deeply cared about. And I was embarrassed to admit all of this to Bob.

For months I'd worked hard to rescue my babies by using my stockpile of "conventional arms"—the frontal and reasonable approach I'd always relied upon to win my personal wars. So I'd already spent many hours in close combat with this man, who was much older and more experienced than me, firing off the kind of honest, openhearted, and earnest arguments that almost always "worked" for me. Like you, I know that most people in most conversations respond to honest arguments, most of the time. But not this time. And I was getting more and more angry and frustrated as the truth about what was going to happen sank in. I was clearly losing the battle, and I'd already used all the bullet-arguments in my bandolier. Meanwhile, that wry little grin on this guy's face had a menace behind it, like the look of a predator that's just spotted its next meal.

And that's when it dawned on me that the direct, frontal approach that had always worked so well for me my whole adult life, and had won me praise and respect from ministry leaders and friends, was clearly not going to get the job done here. My adversary was willing to engage me in a way that was guaranteed to intimidate me into defeat. Author James Ryle says:

> Don't expect a frontal assault from the enemy. He's
> far too clever for that. He knows that you love and

treasure the Word of God, and that you would not stand for any attack against it. Instead, he sabotages your time and distracts your attention. He preoccupies you with skirmishes on other battlefronts, or he lulls you into complacency with prolonged cease fire. All the while he is feverishly working at cutting you off from communication and supplies. If he succeeds he will win the war![2]

The treatment I was enduring wasn't frontal bullying, really, because shrewdly nefarious people have a knack for following the rules (and never breaking a sweat)—it wouldn't be prudent to leave obvious evidence behind at the "crime scene." Technically, everything my adversary had done was "by the book" and aboveboard. But just under the surface was a conspiracy to commit a kind of murder.

Sure, "murder" is way too melodramatic. But it's not as over-the-top as you might assume. In Matthew 5:21–22 Jesus identifies anger as a form of murder, and in Mark 7:21 He tells us our hearts produce evil thoughts that often include murder, and in John 8:44 He tells the Pharisees that they are "of [their] father the devil" who "was a murderer from the beginning." But, even so, "murder" still sounds pretty damning. Here's the nuance: "murder" also describes the way a cheetah takes down a hobbled springbok at the back of the herd. Yes, it's a premeditated killing, but that cheetah is hardwired to find food where it can, when it can. It *needs* to eat that springbok to survive. And my adversary *needed* to murder something precious to me to survive—I don't know why survival was on the line for him; I just know that his hungry soul drove him to "kill and eat." And just as the predatory "angel of light" (2 Cor. 11:14) wears a little grin, not a snarl, when he does his killing, stealing, and destroying, those who use the tools of shrewd to tear apart their "prey" appear complacent, confident, and in control. Their relaxed, even delighted, demeanor is intended to crush their prey's hope. I love the way Mick Jagger's snarling timbre describes this phenomenon in "Sympathy for the Devil":

> *Please allow me to introduce myself;*
> *I'm a man of wealth and taste.*
> *I've been around for a long, long year,*
> *Stole many a man's soul and faith....*[3]

In repeated confrontations I tried to keep my adversary from taking down baby #2. But I was losing ground, and that menacing little grin was getting to me. Then, after a particularly frustrating encounter, the shock of what was about to happen jolted me into a foreboding truth—I'd have to do something that seemed rather … ugly … if I wanted to save the day. That's why, sitting there at Panera Bread, I felt so embarrassed and exposed—I knew I had no idea, not even a starting point, for engaging someone who was a master mechanic wielding the wrench of shrewd.

I told all of this to my friend Bob as he sipped his coffee and nodded his head. I told him that Jesus had rescued me out of a life of posing and hiddenness and shame, and that nothing was more of an expression of my redeemed life than my frontal—open, vulnerable, authentic—approach to relationships. I told him that, like the Olympic sprinter Eric Liddell in the film *Chariots of Fire*, I "felt the Lord's pleasure" when I engaged the people in my life barefaced, with courage and boldness. I told him that I knew God enjoyed all this about me. And then I told him, finally, the kicker—that I had sensed God metaphorically putting His arm around me, then leaning in to reveal a sobering truth:

> *Son, I love who you are and what you've become, but your frontal approach just won't cut it anymore—not in the dark corners of life where I desperately need you to go. Your adversary will surely kill your baby unless you learn how to move shrewdly against him.*

I told Bob about this challenge with the kind of embarrassment that a boy has when he realizes he needs to step up and be a man, but he's not sure if he really is one. And then Bob did something that shocked me—he leaned back in his seat and let out a howl of laughter, delighted in the moment. And he said, eagerly: "Rick, I couldn't agree more with what you've just said. It's *crucial* that you lay down your frontal approach in this confrontation and learn how to be shrewd … *right away*. You've approached this challenge head-on, and you're going to have to go sideways."

Sideways, he said. *Sideways.* I knew it was true as soon as he spoke it—Shrewd = Sideways. But what to do with that? If the practice of shrewd meant that I must reexamine my "frontal" strategies and learn how to move obliquely, it also meant I must reexamine my assumptions about right and wrong. For example, in the Christian community, we tend to criticize what people in the world say they want—wealth, fame, sex, power—and leave it at that. What they want is not good for them because it's sin, so our goal becomes to convince them to give up what they want and accept what we would like them to receive instead—the gospel of Jesus Christ. Effectively, we ignore or diminish or dismiss the door they're leaving open because it would be wrong for us to walk through that door. A sideways approach, instead, would mean that we humble ourselves to enter through the *portal of their want* with the shrewd-but-innocent intention of leading them to what Jesus says they need most.

The apostle Paul was well acquainted with the "sideways" approach—here, in 1 Corinthians 9:20–23, he offers up his manifesto:

> To the Jews I became as a Jew, that I might win Jews;
> to those who are under the Law, as under the Law,
> though not being myself under the Law, so that I
> might win those who are under the Law; to those
> who are without law, as without law, though not
> being without the law of God but under the law of
> Christ, so that I might win those who are without
> law. To the weak I became weak, that I might win
> the weak; I have become all things to all men, that
> I may by all means save some. I do all things for the
> sake of the gospel.

Yes, Paul practices the art of shrewd "for the sake of the gospel," but his account doesn't deliver its disturbing impact unless we translate it into language that's culturally equivalent:

> And to the far-left politicians I became as a far-left
> politician, that I might win far-left politicians; to

those who are far-right fundamentalists, as embracing
far-right fundamentalism; to the cross-dressing gay
prostitutes on Sunset Boulevard, as a cross-dressing
prostitute, though not as a "practitioner" but as a
Christ-follower, that I might win those who are selling themselves on the streets. To the meth addicts I
became like a meth addict, that I might win the meth
addicts; I have become all things to all people, that
I may by all means save some. I do all things for the
sake of the gospel. (author's paraphrase)

Here, there are echoes of John Kay's central description of
obliquity: pursue your "high-level objectives" by experimenting with
"pragmatic improvisation in the face of circumstances." Sideways
is not only counterintuitive, but it's also risky and hard and upset-
ting to our sensibilities. And why wouldn't it be? The redemption
of God's beloved creation—you and I—is no walk in the park. War
is hell, and Paul leaves no doubt that we are at war: "For though
we walk in the flesh, we do not war according to the flesh, for the
weapons of our warfare are not of the flesh, but divinely powerful
for the destruction of fortresses. We are destroying speculations and
every lofty thing raised up against the knowledge of God, and we
are taking every thought captive to the obedience of Christ" (2 Cor.
10:3–5). Weapons, war, and destruction—the Christian life is nothing like the spiritual spa treatment it's become for much of Western
Christianity; it's more like a firefight on the streets of Kandahar.
Bluntly, Paul describes his everyday life experiences with a kind of
mercenary glee:

Five times I received from the Jews thirty-nine lashes. Three times I was beaten with rods, once I was stoned, three times I was shipwrecked, a night and a day I have spent in the deep. I have been on frequent journeys, in dangers from rivers, dangers from robbers, dangers from my countrymen, dangers from the Gentiles, dangers in the city, dangers in the wilderness, dangers on the sea, dangers among false brethren; I have been in labor and hardship, through many sleepless nights, in hunger and thirst, often without food, in cold and exposure. (2 Cor. 11:24–27)

Of course, "received … thirty-nine lashes" is just another way of saying he was beaten within an inch of his life, because the whip that was used on him was studded with sharp barbs. And, moreover, stoning was typically a form of capital punishment, and few sailors in Paul's time survived even one shipwreck, let alone three. Paul lived in constant danger from both enemies and camouflaged friends. His "normal Christian life" makes my normal Christian life look like a stroll down Sesame Street. That's because Paul, one of the shrewdest men in history, was determined to engage his adversary using the kind of forceful leverage that will rivet your enemy's attention on you. In fact, when I began using shrewd leverage to rescue my "baby" from the death sentence it was living under, my adversary's little grin disappeared—it was replaced by a grimace and then a growl and then a snarl. Now that I was no longer unwitting prey for him to consume, we were engaged in outright hostilities—me continuously experimenting with new forms of leverage; him increasingly blowing up at me, both in public and in private. On the fly, I was trying to create and implement my own little counterinsurgency "surge."

After many years of war in Iraq and Afghanistan, experts in counterinsurgency have learned that long-term success depends almost entirely on soldiers embedding themselves in the streets and villages that have been overrun by the enemy. The goal is to infect the locals, through close and ongoing relationships, with a desire to reject the influence and presence of the insurgents. General David Petraeus, former commander of American forces in Iraq and, later, in Afghanistan, describes his strategy:

> You don't end an industrial strength insurgency by killing or capturing all the bad guys. You have to kill, capture, or *turn* the bad guys, and that means reintegration and reconciliation. In the case of Iraq, we reconciled with tens of thousands. It was, in Iraq, a major decision. We were actually going to sit down with individuals who had our blood on their hands and talk about reconciliation. Again, you're not going to kill or capture your way. Military action is absolutely necessary, but it is not sufficient.[4]

This is just another way of saying that frontal approaches are necessary but not sufficient—we must learn how to also move sideways if we hope to succeed.

Jesus modeled this counterinsurgency strategy in a big way—we like to call it the incarnation. As Eugene Peterson so playfully and eloquently puts it in his translation of John 1:14—"The Word became flesh and blood, and moved into the neighborhood" (MSG). And Jesus underscores this "embed" strategy by describing Himself to the Pharisees as a doctor to the sick (Matt. 9:12) who hobnobs with known and obvious ne'er-do-wells so often that He's accused of being a "glutton and a drunkard, a friend of … 'sinners'" (Matt. 11:19 NIV). It's no accident that God chose Gamaliel's prodigy to embed the gospel around the known world and to write most of the New Testament. But Paul did not create the sideways approach ("I have become all things to all people, that by all means I might save some"—1 Cor. 9:22 ESV)—he learned it from the Sensei of Shrewd Himself.

The Heart of the Wolf

Jesus told the Parable of the Shrewd Manager specifically because He knew His followers—you and I—were woefully unprepared to face the real challenges of advancing the kingdom of God on earth. That's because we're advancing this kingdom in the shadow of Mordor, to co-opt Tolkien's *Lord of the Rings* metaphor for the kingdom of darkness ruled by Lucifer. We are, remember, "as sheep in the midst of wolves" (Matt. 10:16). And we've already acknowledged that sheep in the wild stand no chance—*no chance*—against a pack of wolves. Because Jesus always chooses the perfect metaphor to describe our reality, it's worth digging deeper into the habit patterns of wolves. In their forest habitats, wolves achieve a very low yield on their hunting expeditions—they successfully kill their prey only rarely (somewhere between 4 and 8 percent of the time). In contrast, lions have a kill rate of 27 percent or more. This means that wolves are opportunistic hunters. If they sense an unusually good opportunity to kill, they often go after more than they can eat in one sitting. The pack will return again and again to their kill—they're rarely wasteful. Because a wolf's favorite prey species—deer, elk, moose, and caribou—can mortally wound them with one swift kick, wolves focus on the most vulnerable in their target group.

But sheep, unlike their wild ungulate cousins, have no defense whatsoever against wolf attacks. So they are quickly dispatched if they are not protected from them. They are utterly, profoundly at the mercy of their shepherd's skill in fighting off every deadly threat. And this (THIS!) is how Jesus sees us as we venture out into a razor-toothed world. If we are not shrewd, Jesus warns, we stand no chance against the carnivorous momentum of the one who "prowls around ... seeking someone to devour" (1 Peter 5:8). We cannot match our Enemy's teeth, but God has provided us with both defensive protection ("Put on the full armor of God, that you will be able to stand firm against the schemes of the devil"—Eph. 6:11) and offensive weapons ("For though we walk in the flesh, we do not war according to the flesh, for the weapons of our warfare are not of the flesh, but divinely powerful for the destruction of fortresses"—2 Cor. 10:3–4). And our primary "not of the flesh" weapon is innocent shrewdness.

Jesus knew that "the weapons of our warfare" would be counterintuitive to us and hard for most to learn. So He tries to make Himself clear (not an everyday practice for Him). Planted in the midst of His own pack of predators whose names are "the Pharisees and teachers of the law," Jesus turns to His disciples and tells them a startling, scandalous, but crystal-clear story—a story that challenges everything we think we know about Him. He chooses His words, and His setting, well. He's essentially pointing to the "pack" circling Him and outlining exactly how to defeat its tactics and physical superiority. The problem is that the story is so repellent to us that we don't know what to do with it. So we go to great lengths to make excuses for Jesus's strange choice of heroes.

Study the notes on Luke 16 in your Bible, or go the extra mile and pull that dusty commentary out of your bookcase, and you'll discover that the Parable of the Shrewd Manager makes smart, insightful people positively squirm. It's not possible, they say, that Jesus was lifting up this shady—even evil—character as an example for us. Maybe the guy didn't *really* cheat his master; maybe he just cut his "commission" from these deals to ingratiate himself with his master's debtors. Or maybe Jesus was praising the outcome of this story and not the man himself. On and on, smart people feel the need to explain away what Jesus did by using this ... *snake* ... as an example for us—as if they're embarrassed by Him.

Many contemporary translations of the Bible choose to deal with our collective dissonance over the Parable of the Shrewd Manager, and our collateral embarrassment, by softening the meaning of the Greek word *phronimos* into "wise" or "prudent" or "subtle." It's true that *phronimos* is used seventeen times in the New Testament and is sometimes translated as "wise." But paired with the word *snake* (again, the same word He uses to reference Satan), it's clear that Jesus's intent was to convey shrewdness or craftiness. That's why the New International Version, the New Living Translation, the Good News Translation, and others render the word as "shrewd," not wise (Eugene Peterson, in his paraphrase *The Message*, pushes the envelope even more by translating the word as "crooked"). In Genesis 3:1, the word shows up when the Enemy in the garden is described as "crafty."

Instead of explaining away Jesus's choice of words, and His obvious purpose in highlighting the behavior of the shrewd manager, what if we took Him at face value and asked ourselves: what is He hoping we'll learn from the way Satan outwits, outplays, and outlasts the children of God? He offers us His own behavior as an answer to that question—giving us plenty of examples from His own encounters with the wolf pack. For example, when the henchmen of Herod (the man Jesus calls "that fox" in Luke 13:32), show up to "catch him in his words" (Mark 12:13 NIV), they throw a shrewd challenge in His lap that feels like the first move in a chess match:

> They came to him and said, "Teacher, we know you are a man of integrity. You aren't swayed by men, because you pay no attention to who they are; but you teach the way of God in accordance with the truth. Is it right to pay taxes to Caesar or not? Should we pay or shouldn't we?"
>
> But Jesus knew their hypocrisy. "Why are you trying to trap me?" he asked. "Bring me a denarius and let me look at it." They brought the coin, and he asked them, "Whose portrait is this? And whose inscription?"
>
> "Caesar's," they replied. Then Jesus said to them, "Give to Caesar what is Caesar's and to God what is God's."
>
> And they were amazed at him. (vv. 14–17 NIV)

Yes, the Herodians are amazed because Jesus moves sideways instead of frontally, outsmarting and checkmating the wolf pack barely a minute into their encounter with Him. The word translated "hypocrisy" here is the Greek word *hupokrisis*—its literal meaning is "stage-playing." It means these connivers are simply "putting on a face" to trick Jesus into thinking they're impressed with Him and are on His side. But He knows His enemies intend to leverage Him by using a string of false compliments as a preamble to administering their coup de grâce. And Jesus doesn't take their bait. Instead of delivering an answer that's sure to offend the Jews (who treat fealty to Caesar as an act of betrayal to God) or sure to incense the Romans (who are always on high alert for rebel leaders who deny the authority of Caesar), He offers a shrewd response that neither side can leverage. In one turn of His wrench, He acknowledges both the authority of human government and our higher obedience to God. The sheep, it turns out, has fangs—living out in real time the closing lyric to King David's song of worship in Psalm 18: "To the faithful you show yourself faithful, to the blameless you show yourself blameless, to the pure you show yourself pure, but to the crooked you show yourself shrewd" (vv. 25–26 NIV).

We Don't Have What We Must Have

At the end of the Parable of the Shrewd Manager, Jesus delivers a bombshell indictment: "For the people of this world are more shrewd in dealing with their own kind than are the people of the light" (Luke 16:8 NIV). The world is brimming with case studies that prove His point, including one that involves a poor black girl from rural Mississippi who survived a rape when she was nine and gave birth to a son (who later died in infancy) when she was just fourteen. This disadvantaged and disenfranchised girl would later become the most influential woman in the world, presiding over the highest-rated daytime talk show in US history while becoming the richest African American of the twentieth century. Her name, of course, is Oprah Winfrey. But how did she get from *there* to *here*? There are many ways to answer this question. But overshadowing them all is a simple truth: Oprah studiously learned the art of shrewd.

Not long ago a friend of mine, who helped construct and outfit the headquarters for the new cable channel OWN, told me a story that he heard firsthand from one of Oprah's famously loyal lieutenants. During construction, Oprah and her foot soldiers met with a team of professional decorators to choose the artwork that would adorn the new building's walls. After the decorators offered up their best ideas, one after the other, Oprah was not happy. Abruptly, she asked the professionals to leave the conference room. When the door closed behind them, Oprah turned to her loyal employees and smiled. "This is a creative company," she began, "expressly because we value creativity from the top to the bottom. That means all of you are in this room because of your creative ability. And I don't like anything I just saw—it just didn't feel right for us. So, because you're all such creative people, I want *you* to create the artwork that will go on these walls. Do anything you want, but push yourself creatively. Whatever you create we'll put up. Go to it!"[5] And they did—the walls that enclose Oprah's media empire are today adorned with the creative fruits of her staff, who surely had a craft party for the ages.

Locked up in this little vignette is the "secret shrewd sauce" in Oprah's recipe for world domination. Study what she said to her employees as if it were a textbook on everyday shrewdness, and you'll discover that Oprah …

- found a way to turn her corporate headquarters into a more intimate, personal, and unique environment;
- fueled loyalty in her staffers by communicating her unabashed belief in them;
- communicated her decisive leadership, and that she'll "go to bat" for those who are fueling her success;
- modeled a lofty standard of creativity, and reminded her staffers that she expects them to exercise their creativity in every aspect of their job; and
- solidified her reputation as a leader you *want* to follow.

Of course, Oprah did not *plan* to replace her professional decorators with an amateur craft show—that would've been manipulative, not shrewd. She delivered this masterstroke in the moment, without a map, feeling her way forward through the brambles into a brilliant, multilayered stroke of genius. This is just the kind of response that makes the rest of us, after the fact, mumble: "Why didn't I think of that?" That's because it was shrewd, and we rarely see shrewd coming.

And that's exactly why Jesus wants us to study the shrewd "people of this world" like they were textbooks, instead of complaining about them or picketing them or ignoring them or gossiping about them. Jesus is *not* asking us to become evil—like the wicked manager in the parable—for the glory of God; He's asking us to watch how shrewd people—even and especially those we're repelled by—get things done. Shrewdness is merely a certain kind of transmission hooked to a certain kind of engine, and that engine can be evil or good. In the case of Satan, that engine is evil all the time. In the case of Jesus, that engine is better than the best thing you can imagine. Jesus wants us to stay two steps ahead of the one who "kills, steals, and destroys" by exercising our shrewdness. And that means:

1. Most often coming sideways, not frontally— because that's the way Jesus went about "destroying the works of the Devil," and it's the way we will do the same.

2. Studying how things work, then leveraging that system for good, applying the right force at the right time in the right place.

3. Entering in with a dependent attitude. Since we are the branch and He is the Vine, our path forward is to yield ourselves to Jesus and thus share in His shrewdness.

4. Listening in a context of readiness to act. It's up to us to ask God, "What's the shrewd path here?"—then listen, and then act. In truth, this is like learning to dance the tango in our life—to act and speak and move in the same way we respond to the passionate nuances of

a dance partner. It's a *feel* that we react to by experimenting with leverage.

Following the nudges is a subtle art—God whispers because He wants to draw us near. If He shouted we'd *never* have to draw near. And when we draw near He will, like Gamaliel, train us in the habit patterns of shrewd. On a personal prayer retreat I heard God whisper to me: "Sometimes the wind is there to set your face against; sometimes the wind is there to catch and propel you. Ask Me why the wind is in your life today." For the sheep to turn the tables on the wolves, we'll need to pay much better attention to the Shepherd, following His lead and trusting in His love for us. And we will need to move toward and into people and situations, not hang back a polite distance away. We will have to play the instrument, not merely listen to it on our ear buds. We will have to risk stirring the waters in someone, rather than sitting on the shore, waiting to see what happens. We will use the same weapon that Satan uses to kill, steal, and destroy, but we will use it to bring life instead of death.

In a tipping-point scene from *Schindler's List*, Steven Spielberg's much-honored paean to the defeat of the shrewd-and-evil by the shrewd-and-innocent, the industrialist turned savior-of-Jews Oskar Schindler uses shrewdness to convince Amon Goeth, the evil commandant of the Kraków-Płaszów forced labor camp, that it is more powerful to pardon his prisoners than to execute them. Schindler advises Goethe:

> They fear us because we have the power to kill
> arbitrarily. A man commits a crime, he should know

better. We have him killed, and we feel pretty good
about it. Or we kill him ourselves, and we feel even
better. That's not power, though, that's justice. That's
different than power. Power is when we have every
justification to kill—and we don't. That's what the
emperors had. A man stole something, he's brought
in before the emperor, he throws himself down on
the ground, he begs for mercy, he knows he's going
to die ... and the emperor pardons him. This worth-
less man. He lets him go. That's power.... That is
power.[6]

Can you see the turn of the wrench in the hand of Oskar
Schindler? By studying how things work in Goeth's soul (the exercise
of power over others is his addiction), then entering through the
portal of his want (to see himself as a powerful man), then persisting
as he turns the wrench, Schindler moves the immovable. This is how
innocent people, like sheep, fend off and defeat the wolves of the
world. And in my own story, messy as I am, it is how I fended off my
adversary and managed to save baby #2.

On the very day I felt too tired to continue my war of shrewd,
when I was ready to throw in the towel and acquiesce, I discovered
that earlier that same day my adversary had already withdrawn from
the fray, too exhausted to pursue his aim any longer. He offered an
explanation to others that gave him cover for his retreat, but I knew
inside that my experiments with leverage had frustrated him and
sapped him of his will to go on. I realized in that moment that most
shrewdly self-centered people have acclimated themselves to people

who generally offer little resistance. Because of this, they're soft—and that softness is exposed when they're heartily engaged by someone who is innocently shrewd. This same dynamic was at work in the mother of all shrewd encounters—when the Trinity plotted the over-throw of "the ruler of this world," winning back God's beloved from the kingdom of darkness. When Jesus willingly gave up His life as a sacrifice for all, defeating the claims of Satan and stripping him of his authority and power, He knew His Enemy had grown soft after countless millennia spent killing, stealing, and destroying with only spotty resistance. Though the sacrifice was inestimable and the pain was incalculable, it was a relatively easy turn of the wrench for the Sensei of Shrewd.

Bringing the Wood

We are redeemed and released and reborn because a shrewder-than-shrewd Jesus "brought the wood" in His death match with Satan. And it is this willingness to use the right force for the job that distinguishes those who are accomplished practitioners of shrewd. The thirteenth-century Mongol warrior Subutai is, perhaps, the greatest military general who ever lived. A contemporary of Ghengis Khan, Subutai pioneered an approach to siege warfare that made liberal use of engineers on the battlefield. At the decisive Battle of Mohi in Hungary, Hungarian warriors with crossbows turned back the marauding Mongols from an attempted bridge crossing during the night. So Subutai ordered the warriors manning his huge stone throwers to take up positions on his side of the river—these siege engines were not designed for field warfare, but Subutai used them to clear the opposite bank of crossbowmen, opening a way for his light cavalry to cross the bridge and attack the enemy. While the Hungarian warriors were thus occupied by boulders falling from the sky and cavalry surging over the bridge, Subutai's men constructed a makeshift bridge downriver, outflanking their enemy. These tactics— using siege engines tactically on the field and attacking the enemy sideways instead of mounting a frontal attack—were revolutionary at the time, and the well-armed Hungarians had no defense against them.

Subutai always adjusted his warfare strategies to target a particular foe's weaknesses, the unique battlefield terrain, and the changing weather. His goal was to leverage his enemies into a position of weakness *before* his forces attacked. And, in a telling difference between Subutai and his European counterparts, the Mongols emphasized shrewd strategic ability over personal heroism. Western generals such as Richard the Lionheart made a name for themselves by riding to battle at the head of their column of horsemen. But Subutai would typically hang back from the battle, sitting on a hill overlooking the conflict where he could direct the battle using signal flags. He was rarely defeated because he shrewdly positioned his enemy for defeat before the battle began, then adjusted his tactics on the fly as he experimented with leverage and gauged the response.[7]

Like the conniving manager in Jesus's parable, Subutai is not a conventional role model—the Mongols were brutal invaders who practiced genocide on a scale that makes what the Nazis did pale in comparison. In the year 1246, at the height of the Mongol onslaught through Asia and Eastern Europe, the Pope's own envoy to the Great

Khan, John of Plano Carpini, wrote this account of the carnage he witnessed in Russia:

> They [the Mongols] attacked Russia, where they
> made great havoc, destroying cities and fortresses
> and slaughtering men; and they laid siege to Kiev,
> the capital of Russia; after they had besieged the
> city for a long time, they took it and put the
> inhabitants to death. When we were journeying
> through that land we came across countless skulls
> and bones of dead men lying about on the ground.
> Kiev had been a very large and thickly populated
> town, but now it has been reduced almost to noth-
> ing, for there are at the present time scarce two
> hundred houses there and the inhabitants are kept
> in complete slavery.[8]

Carpini's account of a decimated Kiev has the lingering stink of Satan on it—the same way campfire smoke stays embedded in your clothes for weeks. Obviously, nothing about Subutai or the Mongol "Golden Horde" is worth emulating in a life dedicated to following Jesus … except for the shrewd way Subutai and other Mongol gener-als engaged their enemies. The specific reason Jesus instructed His disciples to be "as shrewd as [Satan]" is that the forces of darkness have learned quite well how to leverage their enemies, since shrewd leverage is their only real weapon. We're to learn shrewd from evil because evil has practiced it most often, and Jesus knows the chil-dren of God have not learned well how to practice it "innocently."

It's the tactics, not the heart, we're to pay attention to—translating the "what and the why" of Subutai's battle strategy into redemptive resolve. Jesus, long before Subutai, conquered the rulers of this world by outfoxing and outflanking them. He used the "defeat" of crucifixion as a ruse to surprise His Enemy and steal back the authority he had first claimed through the betrayal of Adam and Eve. Never before, and never since, has there been such a crushing defeat. And now He wants to free us to likewise "bring the wood" in our everyday encounters, when force is what's required.

A couple of years ago I was in Canada, leading a mix of adults and teenagers through my Jesus-Centered Ministry experience. In one section of the experience, small teams work through a series of Scripture passages that are intended to introduce them to "the Jesus they never knew." At the end of this process I ask groups to finish this statement: "Jesus is …" They can finish it any way they want, based on their exploration of Jesus through Scripture. As group after group calls out their "Jesus is" statements, I write them on a huge sheet of poster board at the front of the room. It's a profound and surprising and even life-changing experience for many. On this day, I was about halfway through the room when a young girl sitting at a table with two other teenagers stood up and proclaimed in a loud voice: "Jesus is a badass." Then she sat down. There was what you might call a pregnant pause, and then the room (full of *very* conservative adults from a *very* conservative denomination) exploded in delighted laughter. I couldn't stop smiling as this prim-and-proper gathering of buttoned-up ministry people spontaneously applauded the teenager's statement—I think they appreciated the raw (and slightly profane) truth of what they'd just heard. I told the girl that I'd never given a reward for an answer in any of my training experiences—ever—but that day was an exception.

I think a fair reading of the Gospels, with preconceived assumptions suppressed, would result in a similar "Jesus is ..." statement for anyone who has the courage (or the adolescent chutzpah) to say it. The shrewdly innocent Jesus is, to borrow from Jim Croce, "the baddest man in town." But His form of bad is *good—better than good*. And that's because His innocence infects every aspect of His shrewdness. If our shrewdness lacks "the innocence of the dove," then it is evil. This is the message embedded in the apostle Paul's most famous work of poetry:

> If I speak with the tongues of men and of angels, but do not have love, I have become a noisy gong or a clanging cymbal. If I have the gift of prophecy, and know all mysteries and all knowledge; and if I have all faith, so as to remove mountains, but do not have love, I am nothing. And if I give all my possessions to feed the poor, and if I surrender my body to be burned, but do not have love, it profits me nothing. (1 Cor. 13:1–3)

Likewise, if we move toward others with shrewd intent but do not have love (or innocence), we are no different than the enemies of God, who use the levers of shrewd to manipulate and destroy. If we are as shrewd as Subutai or Old Man Potter or Oskar Schindler, but do not act in innocence, it profits us nothing.

Chapter 6

The Engine of the Dove

Tell me … do you not feel a spirit stirring within you that longs to know, to do, and to dare—to hold converse with the great world of thought, and hold before you some high and noble object to which the vigor of your mind and the strength of your arm may be given? Do you not have longings like these, which you breathe to no one, and which you feel must be heeded, or you will pass through life unsatisfied and regretful? I am sure you have them, and they will forever cling round your heart until you obey their mandate. They are the voices of that nature which God has given you, and which, when obeyed, will bless you and your fellow-men.
—James A. Garfield, twentieth president of the
United States, in a letter to a friend

A sight of His death—if it is a true sight—is the death of all love of sin.
—C. H. Spurgeon, "The Bitterness of the Cross"

*We all long for [Eden], and we are constantly glimpsing it: our
whole nature … is still soaked with the sense of "exile."*
—J. R. R. Tolkien, *The Letters of J. R. R. Tolkien*

*There is NO SECURITY in what God is doing.
There is only security in WHO GOD IS.*
—Graham Cooke, "The Nature of God"

Here's something imperative, something that is right now burning
the back of my throat:

> *Everything I've said to this point amounts to manipula-
> tion apart from a commitment to live and breathe and
> move innocently, deferring to the Spirit of Jesus in all of
> our "plotting."*

For example, what if the girl I've called "Cammie" in the first pages
of this book actually heard about our plot to lure her to a church function? What would I say to this girl when she asked if the "Cammie"
in the story was really her? And how would I answer her when she
told me how hurt and offended she was by our "plotting"—that it
sounded merely manipulative? Well, I think I'd tell her that the *reason
behind* my daughter's strategic invitation was the crucial thing to pay
attention to—that Lucy loves her and doesn't want her to destroy her
life by continuing down a path that will never give her what her heart
longs for. I'd tell her that all of our efforts to strategize a way around
her defenses were actually a costly gift of love to her, and that our
tactics were subjugated to and boundaried by goodness—by *innocence*.

Shrewdness is a high-powered engine, but its impact can be life-giving or life-destroying, depending on the "transmission" we link to it. I mean that Jesus pairs shrewdness with innocence the same way we pair a scalpel with seven years of medical school, or an M-16 semiautomatic rifle with nine weeks of basic training, or a Cessna 150 with forty hours of flight training and a pilot's license, or a vial of Botulinum Toxin Type A (Botox) with a .1-milliliter push from a syringe. A dangerous thing that could easily bring death and destruction is, instead, used to bring freedom and rescue and even beauty—through practiced restraint. And in the case of shrewd, the *practiced restraint* that must be applied to the right force at the right time in the right place is … "innocence."

Many Bible versions translate *akeraioi*, the Greek word for innocence, as "guileless." Freedom from guile is the crucial differentiator between the evil and innocent applications of shrewd. People who have guile are "insidious" and "cunning in attaining a goal"—they are "crafty" and practice "artful deception" and "duplicity." Guileless people, on the other hand, are like Nathanael, the early disciple who sarcastically asks, "Can any good thing come out of Nazareth?" when he's invited by Philip to come meet Jesus for the first time. And when Nathanael reluctantly agrees to make the trek to see this young rock-star rabbi, he is, in turn, greeted by Jesus with this proclamation: "Behold, an Israelite indeed, in whom is no guile!" (John 1:43–51 KJV). In a gathering storm of fickle crowd-worship, Jesus delights in Nathanael's lack of guile—this young and unaffected man tells it like it is, without the celebrity-worshipping momentum of a closet suck-up. Guileless people are "innocent and without deception." Apparently, that doesn't preclude them from using sarcasm….

The conundrum here is obvious and confusing: the definition of *guile* looks a lot like the definition of *shrewd*. They seem to be synonyms. So how can Jesus tell us we must be shrewd, as long as we don't act with guile? It's as if He's telling us to fire a gun without pulling the trigger. Embedded in this dichotomy is the key to living as a shrewd person (the kind of person Jesus is hoping we'll become) instead of living as a manipulative person (the kind of person Satan is). We are to live shrewdly but innocently—in the spirit of the dove. It's impossible to overestimate or overemphasize this crucial restraint on the levers of shrewd.

My first apartment after I graduated from college was a garden-level bachelor cave strategically located near the complex's swimming pool and tennis courts. Soon after I moved in, I invited my college friend Darren for a visit. On the twenty-seven-second grand tour, I saved my bedroom for last. My single bed was wedged into a far corner of the room, near a window. Directly above my bed on both walls I'd mounted the framed certificates and awards I'd won from high school through college. Darren, with a bemused and delighted smile on his face, said: "Wow, it looks like you've put these up so you can stare up at them when you lie in bed—just to remind yourself of who you are." These words were as sharp as a scalpel to me at the time, but his face and his tone and his spirit showed he'd said them in complete innocence. There was no taste of guile in my mouth. He had no intention of cutting me—in fact, he seemed oblivious to any possible downside to his observation. There was a kind of brutal naïveté to his assessment, and I felt undone and exposed. As soon as he left, and in the wake of his exposure of me, I took all of those framed "immortality symbols"[1] off my walls and put them in a storage box. And that's where they are today. If Darren had *intended* to offend me, I would've reacted defensively. But because his observation had no guile tainting it, I was surgically healed by it—he cut me, but the "innocence" of his approach left no scar. Somehow he fired the gun without pulling the trigger.

Darren's impact on me is a rare experience; we don't often encounter people who can expose and rebuke us without *intending* to be harmful or cutting. That's because innocence and cunning seem mutually exclusive—you're either one or the other, but never both. The dove metaphor Jesus is using references both the Holy Spirit (the same "dove" that descended upon Him after He was baptized in the Jordan River in Matthew 3:16) and its common cultural interpretation as a symbol of love. To the Jews, the dove's beauty and faithfulness to its mate makes it a natural metaphor for human love and innocence. For example, the Song of Solomon says, "My dove in the clefts of the rock, in the hiding places on the mountainside, show me your face, let me hear your voice" (2:14 NIV) and, "Open to me, my sister, my darling, my dove" (5:2 NIV; cf. 1:15; 4:1). In ancient Jewish culture doves were often sacrificed on the temple altar for the propitiation of sins expressly because they represented the most accessible and inexpensive "offering of innocence." Innocence, as embodied in the dove, represents a guileless purity of intent. G. K. Chesterton once wrote: "Let us not be too arrogant about the virtues we cannot help having. It may be that a man living on a desert island has a right to congratulate himself upon the fact that he can meditate at his ease. But he must not congratulate himself on the fact that he is on a desert island and at the same time congratulate himself on the self restraint he shows in not going to a ball every night."[2] Innocence,

Chesterton argued, requires a choice. And to be truly innocent we must have an opportunity that we resist. Real innocence faces evil but remains good.

When we live shrewdly but innocently we are simultaneously "facing evil but remaining good." But the obvious truth is, of course, that none of us is *ever* wholly good—truly innocent and without guile. We're all standing somewhere on the continuum of good and evil, but the end of that continuum, where Jesus is standing, is a galaxy far, far away from our place on the line: "And someone came to Him and said, 'Teacher, what good thing shall I do that I may obtain eternal life?' And He said to him, 'Why are you asking Me about what is good? There is only One who is good" (Matt. 19:16–17a). Jesus is reminding this man, and us, that "good" is defined and exemplified by God, and our assessments of what is good and not good are merely faint echoes of the Trinity's primal core momentum. The man is tossing out "good" to describe Jesus with a kind of nonchalance that exposes his shallow definition of the word. So Jesus hints at a vastly deeper understanding of "good" that overshadows our conventional interpretations.

We long for innocence, but it is always and everywhere out of our reach. We are not good like God is good. The best we can do, according to the prevalent patterns of contemporary Christian practice, is to try harder and harder to be a good person, working diligently to understand and practice God's principles in our life, fueled by our own will to succeed. We intrinsically believe we can gain some measure of "innocence" or goodness by disciplining ourselves to be the best person we can be. The Pharisees were the all-time champions of this pursuit, setting up an elaborate system of "jot and tittle" innocence-management that, if followed, was supposed to guarantee your goodness. And Jesus blasted this system, over and over: "They tie up heavy burdens and lay them on men's shoulders, but they themselves are unwilling to move them with so much as a finger" (Matt. 23:4). The "heavy burdens" He's talking about are "the disciplines of goodness" that we have no hope of shouldering so well that God declares us innocent.

Our burden to live innocently—with utter freedom from manipulation and guilt—typically produces a hierarchy of Christian maturity. We slot those who manage to learn and apply the most "innocence" or goodness at the top of the pecking order, and relegate those who can't seem to muster the discipline necessary for maintaining their innocence to the bottom of the heap. But this pecking order is, in the end, a farce—our dirty little secret is that we know no one, *not a single person*, who's successfully managed to do it. This was Jesus's point with the Pharisees—the people who had worked the hardest and showed the most discipline in following the dictates of man-made innocence. They were utter failures at this enterprise, "unwilling to move them with so much as a finger."

Our failure to live up to the standards we've set for ourselves is obvious—just pay attention to how we talk about "how we're doing" when we gather together. "Well," we say, "of course I'm no Mother Teresa." We fail to realize that even Mother Teresa was no Mother Teresa—she, like all of us, fell short of God's standards for righteousness. As Paul says in Romans 3:23–24: "For all have sinned and fall short of the glory of God, being justified as a gift by His grace through the redemption which is in Christ Jesus." Our justification is a pure gift, not something we can work hard to earn. But that truth doesn't seem to sink in—we're hardwired to live like

Pharisees, hell-bent on *deserving* whatever goodness and innocence is ascribed to us. Because I'm often involved in leading people into a deeper intimacy with Jesus, many have tasted His goodness in a way they've never done before—I'm an accidental midwife for the birth of their renewed passion for Jesus. And, of course, it's not all accident. I do my best to set the stage for this deeper intimacy. Because I have an important role to play in this labor and delivery, it's foundationally tempting to ascribe the goodness they taste in Jesus to the goodness that I wish was intrinsic to me. The overwhelming feelings people have when they encounter Jesus as He really is also splash onto me—and I have a natural drive to want to *deserve* that praise. But I often tell my wife that God has been faithful to graciously humiliate me in these situations, reminding me that it's only in my attachment to Him that I experience goodness flowing through me—the branch that has the life of the Vine running through it. The goodness is real, and it's in me, but its headwaters are in Jesus. On the surface, that's not entirely satisfying to me. The virus that Satan first spread to Adam and Eve—that we can all be little gods if we'll just reject God's authority and seize the authority that is rightfully ours—is the disease that runs through us. We want the credit for our innocence.

And so "grace" functionally becomes merely God's way of winking and looking the other way as we repeatedly fail in our responsibility to grow our own innocence. Again, we know not a *single other person* who's done it—our "heroes" are those who seem to fail a little less than we do. And we flock to read their books and listen to their CDs and go to their conferences because they give us the (false) hope that the utter fantasy we've been led to believe is possible for a few is therefore (theoretically) possible for many. The one obvious problem with this ubiquitous way of thinking is that it would take only a couple of hours spent in close conversation with one of these people (or me, for that matter) to realize they're not even close to producing, on their own, the kind of innocence Jesus is talking about.

Christianity Today columnist Frederica Mathewes-Green writes about "the false gospel of rubber guts," referring to the kind of posing, self-serving displays of "guileless innocence" that so many in the church slide so easily into:

> I was once on a retreat for clergy families, led by the pastor of a large metropolitan church, who would regularly announce he was "putting his guts out on the table" and confessed to low self-esteem and generalized "brokenness."
>
> He never looked more cocky or confident than at those moments; those bursts of confession were, he knew, when his wide-eyed audience was in the palm of his hand.... "You know how novelty shops sell fake rubber 'accidents' to 'fool your friends'?" I complained to my husband. "That guy's got a set of rubber guts."[3]

The message here is that there's a fine line between shrewdness (the redemptive practice that is native to God) and manipulation (the destructive practice that is native to Satan). Under our own strength and direction, we're merely manipulators—offering others our "rubber guts" instead of the shrewdly innocent leverage that produces redemptive impact. But under the guidance and direction of the Holy Spirit, the fountain of all innocence, we are partners with God instead of partners with Satan. Remember in the original *Star Wars* film, when Luke Skywalker stumbles upon a little robot droid that has crash-landed on his distant, forgettable planet, and he responds to the droid's repeated demands to be taken to the old man Obi-Wan Kenobi? There, the droid suddenly begins playing a 3-D video message from a warrior princess named Leia. In it, she desperately pleads for Obi-Wan's help in fighting off the advance of the evil Empire. She ends her frantic message by saying: "Help me, Obi-Wan Kenobi, you're my only hope." That plaintive ending is replayed in the scene, over and over. I've always thought this is such a great battle cry for those who would join King Jesus on His dangerous quest to "proclaim release to the captives, and recovery of sight to the blind, to set free those who are oppressed, to proclaim the favorable year of the Lord" (Luke 4:18–19). We are living in dependent innocence when we repeat, with similar desperation: "Help me, Spirit of God, you're my only hope." We have no real hope in disciplining ourselves to follow biblical principles so well that we develop the innocence we have to have to move shrewdly, without manipulation, toward others. Our only hope is to *attach ourselves to Jesus* and simply maintain that attachment *at all costs*, so we can experience His life and innocence flowing through us. Jesus is the Vine, and we are the branches (John 15:5). We have access to innocence only through our intimate and perpetual attachment to His Spirit.

Of course, all those who call themselves Christian would quickly agree with the diagnosis that we are hopelessly guilty—not at all "innocent"—outside of our attachment to Jesus. But our actions and functional beliefs say the opposite. Even though we *say* we can't do anything on our own to "utterly wipe away our guilt," most often we would rather work harder to earn our own (false and entirely ineffectual) innocence than admit we have little control over it and bind ourselves in a dependent relationship with Jesus. This same reluctance to be intimately joined to God-the-Vine is the common thread running through the people of God, from Adam and Eve to you and me. And this addiction to the drug of our own *deserved* goodness shows up in surprising places….

For example, here's a scene that will be played out thousands of times this Sunday. You're standing in the church foyer or the church hallway or the church parking lot or the church baptismal font, attempting to offer someone a compliment and, instead of receiving your compliment, the person responds with the unsatisfying and nearly argumentative: "Oh, but I'm not nearly as good at (fill in the blank) as I wish I was." Or, the more subversively dismissive: "That wasn't me, that was all God." This sort of interchange happens so often among Christians that it's worthy of satire. *Stuff Christians Like* author Jonathan Acuff writes:

> A few months ago my company had an end-of-the-year holiday party and gave out awards for performance. After the ceremony, my friend Mark said to me, "Tell me the truth, did you believe that you were going to win every one of those awards?" I told him, "Yes, yes I did." Even the ones where the presenter would say, "This lady has a drive that is almost as fiery as her red hair," I thought he was talking about me. "Hey, in the right light maybe my hair

looks kind of reddish and the lady comment could
just be a joke," I thought to myself.

   I think that way because I'm a narcissistic jerk
most days, but the truth is that I hate compliments.
I can't take them. The minute someone says something nice about me I discount it. I say things like,
"Oh that was nothing. Anyone could have done
that." …

   Why are compliments the Christian version of
kryptonite? What makes us so uncomfortable? My
dad told me a story about a minister complimenting
a girl after she sang a song. She blushed and rejected
his words by saying, "That was not me, that was all
God." He responded by saying something like: "I
said it was a good song, I didn't think it was heavenly. No offense, but I think God would have hit
that high note."[4]

What's behind the deflective and dismissive knee-jerk response
most of us have to most compliments? Strangely, our inability to
receive adulation, especially exuberant adulation, is tied to a universal
addiction to our own goodness. We deflect positive feedback because it
feels arrogant to act as if we deserve it. And we must *deserve* everything
we're given because we fundamentally believe it's our goodness, not
God's goodness, that saves us. We're so certain of this that we're often
unwilling to embrace an obvious truth—nothing is ever "all God,"
because God has chosen to partner with us and through us. God is
never "going it alone"—community and partnership are the bedrock

of His nature. God is a Trinity, not a monolith. Our deflection of praise is a diagnostic marker for our lack of innocence. We believe the Great Lie that we can "be like gods," and praise reminds us that this belief is embarrassing to us.

It's counterintuitive, but the reason we treat compliments like kryptonite is that we don't trust our own lurking narcissism. In *A Few Good Men,* when Colonel Jessup (played by Jack Nicholson) screams his now-iconic retort, "You can't handle the truth!" at Lieutenant Kaffee (played by Tom Cruise), he might as well be screaming at all of us. We are full of ourselves, but we desperately don't want to admit it. So we deflect and deny and diminish. It *looks like* we're merely acknowledging our humility and limitations. But if the compliment is essentially true, and we deny or deflect it, then (in obedience to our insecurity) we're calling our encourager a liar. And most of us are a bundle of fibrillating insecurities most days precisely because we believe everything hangs on our goodness—that means we're living in a house of cards, and we sense it.

But people who believe that everything hangs on *God's goodness* are free to receive praise with a kind of eager appreciation. They savor the work and movement of God in their own souls as exuberantly as they savor that work in another's soul. They do not treat achievements as immortality symbols—they know Jesus is their only ticket to immortality. And because they're deeply convinced that no inventory of their own inherent goodness will be enough to barter their freedom, they're free to celebrate the goodness of God that has, truly, made them free. They are openly appreciative of their capabilities but inherently discount the *currency* of capability. Instead, they are impressed with the glory of God seeping out of them. When my daughter Lucy (named after her Narnia alter ego) turned thirteen, she decided she'd have her "party" at our local Ronald McDonald House, making and serving dinner (with help from her friends and Mom and Dad) for fifty-five residents who have critically ill children in a nearby hospital. When I explained to my youth ministry friends what Lucy was planning to do and asked them for creative ways to mark this milestone birthday, two of them responded with "exuberant adulation." The first wrote, "I'm sitting in awe of Lucy—what a true, pure heart," and the second wrote, "I just want to know your secret to raising such a servant-hearted child." It's tempting to dismiss or diminish these sorts of compliments and treat them like kryptonite, because Lucy (and by extension, her parents) is undeserving of such praise. Instead, I responded with this: "She really is an amazing girl who surprises us all the time.... She's a force to be reckoned with." This is, I think, something like the simultaneous "open appreciation of our capabilities" and "discounting of the currency of capability." I can fully appreciate the glory of God in Lucy—the Spirit-influenced "innocence" others sense in her—without worrying about whether she "deserves" the praise directed at her. Grace is an undeserved gift, and so we worship God by celebrating it instead of diminishing it.

"Innocent as doves" people live under the influence and momentum of the Holy Spirit. Their innocence has nothing to do with their own intrinsic goodness—it has everything to do with their dependence on the Spirit, into whose family they are adopted as true sons and daughters, and whose innocence flows through their veins as they maintain their close attachment to Him. That's just another way of saying: "If you abide in Me, and My words abide in you, ask whatever you wish, and it will be done for you" (John 15:7). When you're "abiding," you can ask whatever you wish because it's the Spirit who's influencing your "ask." Abiding is, at its core, simply an expression of intimacy—the Greek word for abide, *meno*, is best translated as "in union." It's not stretching the meaning to say that *meno* has sexual connotations—the union is, as Jesus described, "You, Father, are in Me and I in You, that they also may be in Us" (John 17:21).

Our Sublime Defeat

Not long ago I read that a Christian leader I respect admitted his great temptation in life was to simply "make it happen"—that, instead of trusting God for His timing, he was always advancing, advancing, advancing. I knew exactly what he was talking about. His confession shot through to my core and created an inner conversation that continues to this day.

So, soon after I'd read this leader's admission, I ran into my Panera Bread friend Bob—the director of pastoral staff at my church. I told him about my "make it happen" dilemma, then asked: "How do you know when you've pushed past the line between responsibility and faith into the land of 'make it happen'? I mean, I know God wants me to move into my life with vigor and purpose, but how do you keep yourself from simply forcing things?" Bob smiled, then leaned in and put everything into perspective: "Rick," he said, "if you're looking for a formula you won't find one. It's all about relationship—God is not a fan of formulas. Like I always say, from God's point of view it's always Amos 5:4—'Seek me and live....'"

And there I sat, feeling suddenly restored and exposed and invited. Why do we so quickly lose sight of the orbital center of human existence—that God's deepest desire and every motivation is to restore our intimacy with Him? He wants us to confer with His Spirit about our approach to shrewd, not to depend on patterns and formulas that will effectively replace our need for Him. It's crucial that we understand the DNA of shrewdness, but He wants us to listen to His Spirit for our next move because our motivation must come from innocence—and He is the only source of it. If you're going to be a chess master, you'll need to understand and practice the game. But true masters of the game treat it like the tango—they respond to the slight nuances of the void, trusting a voice they may or may not identify as the Spirit as they move their pieces around the board. God wants to be intimate with us again. But we, just like the generations of God's people stretching all the way back to the garden (where our original father and mother chose the "external hard drive" that the forbidden apple tree offered over "walking in the cool of the evening" with God), seem inclined to prefer the safety of a "thing" over the dangerous intimacy of the Person of God. We are kindred with the Israelites, who begged for the familiar bondage of their Egyptian masters over the unpredictable freedom offered by the Alpha and Omega.

We know exactly why those same Israelites asked Aaron to fashion a golden-calf god for them after Moses went up the mountain to accept delivery of the Ten Commandments. And we might as well nod our heads in agreement when we read that God's people approached Samuel in his old age and demanded: "You are old, and your sons do not walk in your ways; now appoint a king to lead us, such as all the other nations have" (1 Sam. 8:5 NIV). Do we feel any of God's heartbreak when He calms Samuel's outrage toward the Israelites' request with: "Listen to all that the people are saying to you; it is not you they have rejected, but they have rejected me as their king" (v. 7 NIV)? We, and they, are God's heartbreakers. He strips Himself naked on our behalf, offering His heart with matchless vulnerability. And, in cool ignorance, we let Him know we'd prefer the less wild "kings"—the rules and formulas—over the whisper-voice of His Spirit.

We are all the rich young ruler of Luke 18:18–29, who eagerly follows all the rules but spurns Jesus's invitation to intimate relationship because, well, the price is too high. It's a dagger to the heart … and it reminds me of a dream Bob Krulish had about five years ago—it perfectly describes the choice before all of us:

> In the dream I was being pulled down a whitewater
> rapid that was a thrashing and torrential river. I was
> thinking, *I am going to die.* I was aware of being *full
> of fear.* In my thrashing about, trying to stay afloat,
> my wrist hit something…. I assumed it was a branch
> in the water. I grabbed it. It turned out to be a "pool
> ladder" handle sticking way out into the river from
> the bank. I pulled myself in, exhausted. I looked
> back at the river thinking, *That was lucky—for sure
> I would have died.* Then I woke up. Adrenalin was
> pulsing through me, and my heart was literally
> pounding. So I just got up (three thirty in the
> morning) and came to church to "keep the Lord

company." While I was thinking about this dream I heard, by faith, "What did you think of the dream?" I thought, *It was fortunate that the ladder handle was there and I was able to get out and save my life.* The Lord said, by faith, "What if I told you the river was Me?" That stunned me at first. Then I said, "I am willing, and will, jump back in … willingly and gladly…. Bring it on. If it's You, I want all of You that You will give me. I trust You for wherever you take me. I'm going to trust and enjoy the ride." And I jumped back into The River.[5]

It's scary and dangerous to jump back into the River because it means submitting to the defeat of our own control and giving ourselves over to the wild and unpredictable guidance of the Spirit of Jesus. We become innocent not by "making it happen" or by following biblical principles so well in our lives that we effectively gain our own righteousness. We become innocent when the "Dove" rules our decisions and actions—again, it is the Spirit's innocence, not our own, that makes us innocent.

And that's really why no growth of innocence can germinate outside of worship—our central response to God's beauty, grace, and goodness that's as close to an unconditional romantic commitment as we can muster. Worship is the bedroom talk of a people who are utterly enamored of their Spouse, who is Jesus Himself. I love the worship music at my church. But about two years ago I started altering one line in a Michael W. Smith song we occasionally sing—it's called "Above All." I relish 99 percent of that song, but this one line was like eating seaweed to me. And when I sang it, I so often felt something like betrayal—like someone who's forced to "confess" his sins at gunpoint. I know that sounds overly dramatic, but I really did have a visceral reaction whenever I was supposed to sing this one little phrase in the song. So, finally, I just stopped singing the line and substituted my own.

Here's the portion of the song that gave me trouble, with the line that choked me in italics: "You lived to die, rejected and alone.… You took the fall, *and thought of me … above all.*"[6] Sounds innocuous. That's why I'm almost embarrassed to admit how worked up I've been about it. But the reason I can't sing that line (and, instead, substitute "and thought of Him … above all") is that it represents for me a pervasive attitude in Christian culture that "it's all about me." Jesus endured the slaughter of the cross out of loving obedience to His Father—I don't think He was envisioning my face when He said, "Into your hands I commit my spirit" (Luke 23:46). Of course, we are loved to the full extent of love as adopted sons and daughters who are "the apple of God's eye." But on the cross Jesus was thinking of His Father "above all." Now, I'm positive Michael W. Smith had no intention of feeding my latent narcissism. But the point is we're so saturated with subtle what's-in-it-for-me messages that we don't notice them when they creep into our worship songs. *Who, really, are we worshipping here?*

I was reminded of all this again while reading an article on the enduring influence of Louie Giglio's Passion conferences. The article charts the growth and impact of Passion—a gathering for young-adult Christians that has changed the worship repertoire of churches all over the world. Passion worship leaders Matt Redman, Chris Tomlin, Charlie Hall, and the David Crowder Band have infiltrated and subverted the me-first atmosphere of today's worship music and substituted "vertical" songs instead. Instead of wallowing in our need, the songs of Passion have refocused our attention on the greatness and goodness of God—our bedroom response to Him. In the article a twenty-one-year-old Baylor student named Taylor Dodgen says, "In some ways, Passion has put the words that people are going to say to God into the mouths of an entire generation."[7] That's so true. Tomlin's "How Great Is Our God," for example, gives me the bedroom language my heart longs for in worship. Worship leads us to attachment to Jesus in the same way (brace yourself) foreplay leads us to intercourse. And it's our marriage to the Spirit of Jesus, and the intimacy we share in that marriage, that fuels our innocence.

The Marriage Bed

The apostle Paul uses the metaphor of marriage to describe both our freedom from "the law of sin and death" (the deceit and destructive impulses characterized by Satan) and our marriage to innocence (the purity and blamelessness characterized by an untainted Jesus). In Romans 7 he describes our relationship with sin as a marriage that we are unable to free ourselves from—in ancient Jewish culture, the woman in a marriage had few rights and no option for divorce, even if her spouse was abusive. Her only way out—her sole hope for freedom—was through the death of her spouse. In Paul's metaphor, *we* are the woman in the marriage, and sin is our spouse. As long as we stay in the marriage, we're ruled by "the law of sin and death"

(Rom. 8:2). The good news of Jesus Christ is that He paid the penalty for sin when He was crucified, and those who give over their lives to Him "die with Him" (2 Tim. 2:11). We are then released from our obligation to our "old spouse" because that spouse is dead—we are free to remarry. And the astonishing truth is that Jesus's name after His resurrection is "Bridegroom"—now that His bride is free, He can't wait to marry us. Paul channels the hopelessness of his former marriage to sin into a raw plea—"Wretched man that I am! Who will set me free from the body of this death?" (Rom. 7:24). He quickly follows this with equally raw gratefulness—"Thanks be to God through Jesus Christ our Lord!" (v. 25).

And so, we remarry, but we quickly discover what every abused spouse learns: we have so long been with sin, obeying its insidious standards and demands, that we struggle to leave behind our habits of mind and heart even though we are remarried and free. There are examples of this truth all around us....

- When Brooks, the old convict in the film *The Shawshank Redemption*, is finally released from a lifetime in prison, he discovers that he's been so acclimated to the structure and rhythms of prison that he can't survive on the outside. Rather than live in the fear his unfamiliar freedom has produced, he commits suicide in his lonely boarding-house room.
- Even though Iraq now has a fledgling democratic government bought by the ultimate sacrifice of thousands of coalition and Iraqi troops, the country is still racked by many of the same self-destructive

habits it learned while under decades of Saddam Hussein's abusive rule and centuries of tribal warfare and corruption. The old "spouse" is gone, but the old patterns of the "marriage" persist.

- I once heard a missionary to Africa describe how his ministry bought the freedom of an entire village of people enslaved to the owner of a nearby brick factory, only to watch with thudding dismay as each person, one by one, re-sold themselves into slavery within two years. They thirsted for freedom, but when they were handed their freedom, they discovered their addiction to slavery was stronger than they realized.

- In my own life, because I grew up feeling, well, *invisible* in my family and therefore afraid of abandonment, I've always had to wrestle with the temptation to control all my relationships to ensure the people I love wouldn't abandon me. Though I am free today in Christ, those old patterns are intoxicating to me. On any given day it can look like I'm living out of two selves—remarried, but living out my old marriage patterns.

This "intoxication" with our old patterns of survival—from when we were living as slaves in an abusive marriage to sin—is what Paul calls "the flesh." And it's our continuing attachment to the flesh that keeps us from living in innocence. When we renounce the old patterns of our slavery to sin and instead embrace the new patterns of intimacy inherent in our marriage to Jesus, we live and breathe and move in innocence. This is evident in the way Paul transitions his teaching about our former marriage to sin into our present marriage to innocence in Romans 8:

> Therefore there is now no condemnation for those
> who are in Christ Jesus. For the law of the Spirit of
> life in Christ Jesus has set you free from the law of
> sin and of death. (vv. 1–2)

The *therefore* here is huge. Those who are not condemned are declared, down to the marrow in their bones, *innocent and free.* But, though profoundly and pragmatically true, this declaration of innocence does not guarantee a life lived in innocence. Many of us are intoxicated by the rutted patterns of our old "marriage" and continue to live out of our own strength—working hard to follow the law and trying with all our might to be "good people" by following God's principles and setting our minds on our own capacity to come through. Under the law of sin and death, we knew we could not trust our abusive spouse, so we trusted ourselves instead. And trusting ourselves is living out of our own strength—living out of the flesh. We are "abiding" in our own determination to be good, not abiding in the One who is already good. But those who, instead, rely on the Spirit of God living inside them—who orient their whole lives toward the reality of Jesus's intimate presence—set their minds on Jesus. In our old marriage, the focus is on ourselves; in our new marriage, the focus is on Jesus—this is why the phrase *in Him* appears thirty-seven times in the New Testament.

My wife and I have a friend who, after she met us, slowly awakened to the perpetually abusive patterns and demands of her domineering, controlling, and verbally violent spouse. The more time she spent in our home, watching and tacitly studying how Bev and I interacted with each other, the more it dawned on her that the abusive patterns that she had acclimated herself to were not "normal"—she could smell the fragrance of a distant country, where "marriage" was not the same thing as "control." We introduced her to the Bridegroom, and she gave her life to Him. At the same time, she started asking us if she should leave her abusive marriage, and I always responded the same way: "You'll know when, and if, it's time to do that." Four years into our relationship, she knew it was time. She left, and the freedom from the abusive patterns of her life was so profound that she felt born again—light in her spirit and free to be who she really is. But, just as Brooks learned in *The Shawshank Redemption* and I've learned as I've wrestled with my "invisible" past, the patterns we acclimate ourselves to are similar to addictions— they are hard to quit. While we were away on vacation, our friend slipped back into the habit patterns of her addiction. By the time we returned, she'd decided to move back in with her husband. Her first night back, she waited until she was sure her husband was asleep and then found a quiet place in her house to call us. "I know I have chosen a slow death," she told us, with whispered resignation. "I know I have chosen Satan over God. I can't help myself." We have not seen or talked to our friend in more than a year, because she is not allowed to have contact with us now.

To leave behind our addiction to the patterns of our old marriage, we will have to treat those old patterns as if they died on the cross with Jesus. Our focus will need to stay riveted on Him, not on ourselves. When I set my mind on working hard to live a good life in my own strength, fueled by my own commitment to keep the tenets of the law and live as a good person, I will find only frustration and failure and death. But if my attention is given over to the Spirit of God living in me, if I listen and wrestle and learn and do what He asks me to do, then I will find life and alive-ness and peace. If, instead, I've set my mind on keeping the law—the pattern of life in my old marriage—trying hard to live out God's principles in my life, Paul says I'll actually develop a spirit of hostility toward Him. I'll be furious because the things I've assumed He's demanding that I do are, in the end, impossible for me to do. If I'm not able to "subject myself to the law of God," why has God told me that I must? What's more, Paul reminds me (Rom. 8:8) that I will never, ever please God with my efforts. It's as if God has set me up to fail. And, as shrewd as He is, this is essentially true. It's the failure I taste when I try to live in my own strength—working under assumptions that I hold on to from my previous slavery to sin—that ultimately drives me to stop trusting myself and start trusting Him. And this is His deepest hope—that I might trust Him, not myself, from now on. He wants all my efforts to bring myself into compliance with His law outside of a relationship with Him to cease, because He wants me to shift my focus from trying harder to knowing Him better, trusting Him more, and abiding more continuously.

We can relax in our newfound innocence because we know we have not earned it and therefore aren't in control of it. Paul spells this out for us:

For all who are being led by the Spirit of God, these
are sons of God. For you have not received a spirit of
slavery leading to fear again, but you have received
a spirit of adoption as sons by which we cry out,
"Abba! Father!" The Spirit Himself testifies with our
spirit that we are children of God, and if children,
heirs also, heirs of God and fellow heirs with Christ,
if indeed we suffer with Him so that we may also be
glorified with Him. (Rom. 8:14–17)

Paul is telling us that we are not slaves, but children—actually part of a royal family better known as the Trinity. And as children, we are heirs of His innocence. Our treasure is inherited, not stolen or scraped together or even earned. It's a given, because we are part of the family. You see hints of our reality in the following interchange between reporter Mary Louise Kelly and the twenty-seven-year-old Saudi princess Ameerah Al-Taweel, wife of one of the richest men in the world, Prince Alwaleed bin Talal. Al-Taweel has been a dangerously outspoken advocate for relaxing the harsh restrictions on women in Saudi Arabia, particularly the longtime ban on driving within the kingdom:

Kelly: … [Y]ou might not suffer the same consequences as an ordinary Saudi woman might, who
is trying to exercise the right to drive or the right
to work.… Realistically, what do you think Saudi
women should be doing to try to push for these
reforms?

> **Al-Taweel:** … I've been a common girl most of my
> life.… I know what it feels like. Nevertheless, I am
> very optimistic about the future.… Ten years ago,
> it was a taboo for a woman to work. And now it's a
> taboo for women to stay home.[8]

As an ordinary commoner speaking out against draconian Saudi traditions, Al-Taweel would almost certainly be jailed, or worse. But as a grafted-in member of the royal family, she has privileges, freedoms, and points of leverage that she has *inherited*, not earned. And she is using her inheritance to push for changes in Saudi society that would've been unthinkable even ten years ago. In the inherited reality Paul is describing for us, we do not work hard all day just to survive under a harsh slave owner. Rather, we've married into God's family and joined the family business, which is called Redemption, Inc. When we answer Jesus's invitation from the bedroom to "know" Him, we find life, and this life will literally transform us, and our transformation will produce fruit, which will look a lot like the fruit of the Spirit. "Fruit," in this context, is just another way of describing the children that are born of our marriage to Jesus. We produce a certain kind of fruit because of Who we're married to—and that fruit tastes like innocence.

This section I've called "The Marriage Bed" is, simply, my paraphrase of the greatest chapter (8) in one of the greatest books of the Bible (Romans). It is Paul's soaring manifesto on the improbable and even impossible reality that we, through our marriage attachment to Jesus, can actually live in innocence. In Eugene Peterson's raw retrospective on his life as a pastor, *The Pastor: A Memoir*, he describes the mission at the core of our calling:

> I saw myself assigned to give witness to the sheer
> *livability* of the Christian life, that everything in
> scripture and Jesus was here to be lived.... [M]y task
> was to pray and give direction and encourage that
> *lived* quality of the gospel—patiently, locally, and
> personally ... to see to it that these men and women
> in my congregation became aware of the possibilities
> and the promises of living out in personal and local
> detail what is involved in following Jesus, and to be a
> companion to them as we do it.[9]

Yes, it is true that we can move shrewdly while we're both restrained and invigorated by the innocence of the Dove. *This life is livable.* My friend Hal Goble is a retired (and savvy) businessman who has long since dedicated his life to using the shrewd skills he's learned in the marketplace to advance the kingdom of God. You'd never know it from a casual conversation with Hal, but he is living proof that all of us can live like Jesus—bringing hope and redemption through innocent shrewdness. There are so many examples of this in Hal's life. One day, when I was picking his brain about the mechanics of living shrewdly-but-innocently, I was shocked to learn that he'd been a catalyzing influence in the birth of a huge statewide food ministry called FoodWorks Colorado. He had no interest in singling out himself in this story, but the more we talked about the "innocence engine" of shrewd, he couldn't contain his excitement:

> My daughter Gwen invited us to go with her to an
> inner-city church—really, it was two urban houses

connected together and used as a church. After the service, I watched as everyone attending went down the stairs to the basement. I didn't know what was going on. Soon, one by one, they came up carrying big boxes of food—canned goods, bread, and so forth. I asked someone, "Where is all the food coming from?" And a guy answered: "We have three or four guys who volunteer to go to Safeway every week and get their expiring food. We get food for nothing, and then we offer it to the people who show up for church." And I said: "Why aren't we doing this all over town? Every church could be doing this. After the feeding of the five thousand Jesus told His disciples to pick up all the food scraps that had fallen on the ground and save them to give away—they picked up twelve baskets full. There's a real surplus here that you could tap into on a much larger scale!"

So we started looking for ways to expand the idea metro-wide and find a wider array of sources for food that we could give away. Early on a guy walked into my business—he had a forty-foot trailer full of potatoes that had been rejected because they had too much water in them. He offered his forty thousand pounds of potatoes in exchange for a receipt for the market value for these potatoes. That's a huge tax advantage for him, and so much better than his alternative—dumping the potatoes in the dump. And that was the start of the FoodWorks Colorado food ministry. Now there's a huge warehouse with a line of cooking kettles—they're not only collecting food now; they're creating food. The whole thing is aimed toward the struggling single parent—a fulfill-ment of Jesus's command to take care of widows and orphans. FoodWorks Colorado now puts out seventy-six thousand meals per week. We send a semitruck every week to one of the poorest regions in Colorado—the San Luis Valley. And we send a semitruck every other week to an Indian reserva-tion. Shrewdness gives you the means to deliver goodness.[10]

"Delivering goodness" is yet another way of describing what shrewd looks like when it is filtered through innocence. And Jesus is always and everywhere "delivering goodness," using the leverage of shrewd under the influence of innocence—there's never a moment when He is not motivated by love in His movement toward us. But the great difference in the way He "delivers goodness" to us, compared to the way we love Him or love each other, is that He is fully mature in His love. To the fully mature, love is not a sentiment—it's a force. Paul attempts to describe this fully mature love in his letter to the church at Ephesus: "We are no longer to be children, tossed here and there by waves and carried about by every wind of doctrine, by the trickery of men, by craftiness in deceitful scheming; but speaking the truth in love, we are to grow up in all aspects into Him who is the head, even Christ" (Eph. 4:14–15). Leaving childhood behind means that we are no longer tossed around by the "trickery" and "craftiness" and "scheming" of those who are in the service of God's Enemy. Instead, under the influence and momentum of love, we act like grown-ups who are ready to use the right force at the right time in the right place to advance the kingdom of God—and who do so in a posture that is splayed open before the Spirit of God. Our mission and passion, as reflected in Hal's catalyzing influence in the FoodWorks Colorado ministry, is to act as shrewd conduits for the floodwaters of God's love: "Beloved, let us love one another, for love is from God; and everyone who loves is born of God and knows God. The one who does not love does not know God, for God is love" (1 John 4:7–8).

Jesus is not merely urging us to love as He loves, like a finger-wagging Sunday school teacher. He is not *explaining* the way or *pointing* to the way or *dragging* us onto the way—He *is* the way. We learn how to experiment our way forward as people determined to live innocently shrewd by *remaining in Him*. When we remain in Him, we remain in innocence. Tom Melton once described a ministry trip he took to Cuba—he got lost in the middle of Havana, and his beginner's Spanish left him helpless to communicate. Finally, the stranger who'd been trying to give him directions back to his hotel gave up and said, "I am the way back to your hotel—I'll take you there." Sure, Jesus can point us in the right direction, but most of us will remain confused about how to move more shrewdly (restrained and fueled by innocence) in our lives if all we have is a concept to follow. Ultimately, His only recourse is to point to Himself and say, "I am the Way—follow Me."

The Simple Path to Shrewd Living

I've now had more how-to-walk-shrewdly conversations than I can count with people who have problems or challenges or obstacles in their lives but who've found their conventional approaches have brought only frustration and confusion. I've discovered that my feedback almost always follows the same path. So, here in a little nook (possibly a cranny) in this book, I thought I'd map out that path, just in case we never run into each other....

1. Answer the question: "What do I really want?"
   Jesus had a habit of asking an apparently irritating question of people with obvious needs who approached Him for help: "What do you want?" (e.g., Matt. 20:32; Mark 6:22; Mark 10:36; Mark 10:51; Luke 18:41). It's crucial that we recognize why Jesus thought it so important to ask this question in obvious circumstances—we must know what we really want before we can truly ask in faith.

2. Answer the question: "Is my 'want' born out of innocence? Would I feel just fine asking Jesus for this 'want' if I was face-to-face with Him?" If your answer is yes, commit to staying closely attached to Jesus through this process, opening yourself for feedback every day.

3. Now, spend five minutes brainstorming (either alone or with someone you trust) an answer to this question: "Shrewd living always starts with understanding how things work—so what is my understanding of how this (person, organization, or process) works?"

4. Now, based on your understanding of how things work, spend five minutes brainstorming a point of leverage to go after with a "sideways" approach. See if you can come up with at least two options for your "experiment" with leverage. Are you willing to use the sort of force that will likely be necessary to carry out your approach?

5. Now, try one of your options and debrief the results with someone you trust. Decide whether to continue with that option or whether to try a new approach.

6. Repeat steps #3, #4, and #5 in a continuous loop—until you've landed on "the right force at the right time in the right place."

The Elegant Levers

··

An Expedition of Sorts

You have a much greater chance of succeeding by you choosing
the means that they're not equipped to deal with effectively.
—Dr. Gene Sharp

God does not tell you what He is going to
do; He reveals to you Who He is.
—Oswald Chambers, *My Utmost for His Highest*

The function of freedom is to free someone else.
—Toni Morrison

Can it really be true that Jesus never said or did anything that wasn't shrewd? Well, yes. Whether He's offering blunt love to the woman at the well or tender love to two sisters who are grieving their brother's death or ferocious love to the hypocritical Pharisees, it's impossible to find even a single encounter with Him where shrewd leverage is not in play. Jesus was and is shrewd all the time, with everyone He engages. And that means He is right now acting shrewdly in my life and your life—it's like breathing to Him. *When He breathes in, He is understanding how things work; when He breathes out, He is using that knowledge to apply the right force at the right time in the right place.* In and out, over and over, again and again. And every time He exhales you can smell innocence on His breath. Pick an encounter, any encounter, and you'll see the Sensei of Shrewd at work....

- When Jesus is tempted by Satan in the wilderness, He "outwits, outlasts, and outplays" His Enemy at every turn, responding to a series of sly attempts to leverage Him with a little counterinsurgency: "Man shall not live on bread alone, but on every word that proceeds out of the mouth of God" (Matt. 4:4) and "You shall not put the Lord your God to the test" (v. 7) and "You shall worship the Lord your God, and serve Him only" (v. 10).
- When Jesus is challenged by the conniving Jewish leaders who've dragged a woman caught in the act of adultery before Him, hoping to destroy His mystique and His following, He out-shrewds them all with: "He who is without sin among you, let him be the first to throw a stone at her" (John 8:7).
- When Jesus heals a man's withered hand on a day no God-fearing Jew is supposed to do "work," and the Pharisees try to set a trap for Him by asking,

"Is it lawful to heal on Sabbath?" Jesus responds, "You'd get your sheep out of a pit on the Sabbath, right?" (Matt. 12:10–11, author's paraphrase).

- When the woman with "an issue of blood" (Mark 5:25 KJV) sneaks up behind Jesus in a crowd to touch the hem of his garment, Jesus stops, quiets the crowd, and asks: "Who touched me?" He already knows power had gone from Him—the woman has found the physical healing she's seeking, then melts back into the crowd. But her behavior hints at the shame she's long since acclimated herself to, and Jesus flushes her out of hiding to expose that shame to the light of the crowd, where it burns away and leaves her free in *both* body and soul (vv. 26–34).

- And remember that Canaanite woman who grovels on the floor before Jesus, pleading with him to heal her daughter of demon possession? And remember that Jesus first ignores her and then answers her with what seems like scorn, telling her He's come for the children of Israel, not for "dogs" like her? And remember how, with brilliant tactical desperation, the woman responds with this bit of shrewd leverage: "Even the dogs eat the crumbs that fall from their masters' table" (Matt 15:27 NIV)? And remember how Jesus explodes with delight and praise: "Woman, you have great faith! Your request is granted" (v. 28 NIV)? When you're an Artist working in the medium of shrewd, you're also what Tom Melton calls an *aprecianado*[1] of the art form— you know a prodigy when you see her.

Every dapple of color on Jesus's palette represents a different shade of shrewd on the continuum.

Of course, I recognize that I'm framing all of this as fact rather than earnest conjecture. So, out of deference to the scientific process, a progressive system of exploration that was developed by Galileo Galilei to codify facts, let's move from hypotheses to exploration to results to conclusions. Our starting point is my (obvious) hypothesis that Jesus never did or said anything that wasn't shrewd. To experiment with this hypothesis, we'll closely examine six stories about Jesus—a representative sample—and treat them like organic specimens that we can test for evidence of shrewd....

The Lever of Humility

Listen, my friend! Your helplessness is your best prayer.
—Ole Hallesby, *Prayer*

The Story: "Then Jesus arrived from Galilee at the Jordan coming to John, to be baptized by him. But John tried to prevent Him, saying, 'I have need to be baptized by You, and do You come to me?' But Jesus answering said to him, 'Permit it at this time; for in this way it is fitting for us to fulfill all righteousness.' Then he permitted Him" (Matt. 3:13–15).

The Exploration: Baptism was instituted by God as an outward symbol of an inward reality—it's a symbolic cleansing that marks the complete "washing" of sin from our souls as we confess and repent. So why would a sinless Jesus not only submit to baptism but *ask* to submit to it? He tells John to permit it because "it is fitting for us to fulfill all righteousness" (v. 15). Even though Jesus is the wholly "perfect" embodiment of righteousness, fulfilling and therefore superseding the "partial" and temporary bridge to righteousness that is the Mosaic law, He chooses the path of shocking humility instead. Later, Paul will describe Jesus's attitude toward the outward requirements of righteousness in his apostolic letter to the Christians living in Philippi: "Have this attitude in yourselves which was also in Christ Jesus, who, although He existed in the form of God, did not regard equality with God a thing to be grasped, *but emptied Himself*, taking the form of a bond-servant, and being made in the likeness of men" (Phil. 2:5–7). This *emptying* is a purposeful strategy that is necessary for Jesus to accomplish His redemptive intentions, using the leverage of humility.

In 1797, after George Washington left office as the first US president, he decided to give back his commission as a five-star military general to guarantee that the young republic would not be plunged into a power struggle after its very first peaceable transfer of power. In effect, he *emptied himself* of the trappings of power to lever the country forward into a pattern of democratic succession that he hoped would perpetuate a government "by the people, for the people." It's easy to forget the prevalent and endemic patterns of Washington's day—despotic leaders who clung to power by keeping their people in an eternal state of powerlessness and fear. By choosing to strip himself of all formal power Washington redirected the course of American history away from the common path of authoritarian rule and toward a quarter millennium of democratic freedom.[1]

Hundreds of years later, four-star Army General Peter Chiarelli, second in the army's ranking hierarchy, was attending a swanky Washington dinner at the invitation of President Barack Obama. White House adviser Valerie Jarrett, a longtime Chicago friend of

President Obama, was enjoying her dinner when. Chiarelli (in full-dress uniform) walked past the place she was sitting. She caught a glance of his uniform slacks and mistakenly assumed he was a waiter, so she asked Chiarelli to get her a glass of wine. In the tiny pause that buffered her request she took a closer look at the "waiter" and was mortified when she realized her mistake. In that moment Chiarelli responded by *emptying himself,* quickly finding a bottle and pouring her a glass of wine. In response to her repeated apologies, Chiarelli brushed off the gaffe and invited her to come to dinner at his home at a later date. His response left an indelible mark on Jarrett and the roomful of power brokers who'd witnessed the interchange—true power, as Oskar Schindler shrewdly reminded Commandant Goethe, is expressed when those who could throw their weight around choose not to. And Chiarelli may never have exercised his power with more impact than when he embraced the spirit of a waiter instead of the privileges of a decorated warrior.[2]

The Results: The *emptying* that is inherent in humility is powerfully shrewd on multiple levels. In the example of Jesus, His meticulous adherence to the tenets of the law, even when they had no bearing or impact on Him, allowed Him to roll back all consequences of sin when He took the law and all its obligations and consequence with Him to the cross. Because He was faithful in all things, including those dictates of the law that had no intrinsic application to Him, He left His Enemy no crack or fissure to leverage—"For the ruler of the world is coming, and he has nothing in Me" (John 14:30). Likewise, Washington gave away his power to accomplish something remarkable—outsmart his future self. Let's say things go badly after he leaves office, and the pressure on "Five-Star General Washington" to step back into the presidency grows to a fevered pitch, with the crowds and his allies in the military urging him to bring the familiarity of his authority back into a dangerous chaos. Would he be able to resist the temptation? Maybe, but why leave room for leverage? In chess terms, he sacrificed his queen to save his king, leveraging the republic into a checkmate position for a democratic future. Washington's act of prophetic humility is a clear reminder of the advice Jesus gave when He noticed that the invited guests at a Pharisee's feast were fighting over the places of honor at the table:

> When you are invited by someone to a wedding
> feast, do not take the place of honor, for someone
> more distinguished than you may have been invited
> by him, and he who invited you both will come and
> say to you, "Give your place to this man," and then
> in disgrace you proceed to occupy the last place. But
> when you are invited, go and recline at the last place,
> so that when the one who has invited you comes,
> he may say to you, "Friend, move up higher"; then
> you will have honor in the sight of all who are at the
> table with you. For everyone who exalts himself will
> be humbled, and he who humbles himself will be
> exalted. (Luke 14:8–11)

When and *so that* and *then* and *for* are the buzzwords of shrewd thinking, and Generals Washington and Chiarelli speak its language well.

The Conclusion: When Jesus offers His unsolicited wisdom to the assembled guests at the Pharisee's feast, He is urging them—and us—to use the lever of humility as a matter of habit. When we are tempted by arrogance or self-inflation, we move in humility instead in order to gain redemptive leverage.

The Lever of Blunt

Jesus promised his disciples three things—that they would be
completely fearless, absurdly happy, and in constant trouble.
—G. K. Chesterton

The Story: "Now Saul, still breathing threats and murder against the disciples of the Lord, went to the high priest, and asked for letters from him to the synagogues at Damascus, so that if he found any belonging to the Way, both men and women, he might bring them bound to Jerusalem. As he was traveling, it happened that he was approaching Damascus, and suddenly a light from heaven flashed around him; and he fell to the ground and heard a voice saying to him, 'Saul, Saul, why are you persecuting Me?' And he said, 'Who are You, Lord?' And He said, 'I am Jesus whom you are persecuting, but get up and enter the city, and it will be told you what you must do'" (Acts 9:1–6).

The Exploration: In the midst of His Tony Soprano moment, Jesus is doing more than merely forcing a puffed-up Pharisee off his donkey—He's pushing an immovable boulder down the hill toward the kingdom of God using "blunt-force trauma" to leverage His unsuspecting persecutor. Sometimes the language of blunt—formidable as it is—is the sort of harsh leverage that's necessary to move the immovable. The intrinsic power of blunt leverage reminds me of a story my pastor friend Christie Kelly told me about one of her favorite youth ministry moments: "This is why I love teenagers so much. Last night the middle school girls and I were making Valentine's Day cards for the sick and shut-ins at our church. One of the women we made a card for is terminally ill. We discussed possible things we could write inside. One of the girls thought she had a great idea: 'Let's write—"Praying you are close to God, as you will be seeing Him soon."' Gotta love 'em—they get right to the heart of things!"[1] This middle school girl's proposed valentine to a dying woman feels a lot like the Canaanite woman's response to Jesus after He called her a dog—refreshingly and enjoyably blunt. Jesus certainly responded with surprised delight when He heard, "Even the dogs eat the crumbs that fall from their masters' table" (Matt. 15:27 NIV), and I see no reason He wouldn't be smiling ear to ear when He heard "as you will be seeing Him soon." He is well acquainted with the lever of blunt and enjoys the company of those who use it well.

I have a much better sense of how Paul was impacted by the lever of blunt after meeting fifty-five-year-old Tamrat Layne at a small gathering hosted by author and UCLA philosophy professor Dallas Willard. Tamrat was waiting, just like me, to talk with Willard after his two-hour Q&A session. We introduced ourselves but said little. Later, a mutual friend told me something about the tall, angular black man that shocked me—only months before, he'd been released from an Ethiopian prison after twelve years of solitary confinement. Before that, Tamrat was the communist prime minister of Ethiopia, living in a walled-off luxury home in Addis Ababa. I contacted Tamrat and asked to meet with him. I learned that after many years as a jungle insurgent (he would call himself a "freedom fighter") who'd joined the communist cause when he was just nineteen, he'd been instrumental in ousting Ethiopia's military regime in 1991, later moving into a top leadership position in the Ethiopian People's Revolutionary Democratic Front coalition.

In 1996 his best friend and closest ally—Ethiopian president Meles Zenawi—accused him of corruption and abuse of power, then had him arrested. For six years the jailed Layne fought accusations that he was involved in an illegal sixteen million dollar deal to export Ethiopian textiles and that he used his position to export a thousand tons of state-owned coffee through a bogus firm. In the end, the Ethiopian Supreme Court found Layne guilty and sentenced him to eighteen years in prison. There, he seethed and boiled, plotting his revenge against those who'd betrayed him.

It was during those long days and nights in a dank Ethiopian prison that Tamrat experienced the blunt leverage that would eventually redeem him. In 2002, during a stay in the prison's hospital ward, he says a nurse surreptitiously slid a gospel tract into his hand, risking her job to offer him the hope of Jesus Christ. Tamrat recalls, "That tract had only about four or five lines, but I started asking, 'If You are Jesus Christ,' as the tract explains, 'then come to me and give me a new life.' I had never known the thing called prayer, [but] I spent that whole day praying. Then, the next night while I was sleeping, I woke up suddenly. The room was filled with a brilliant light. From one corner of the room, a man appeared. He said to me, 'I am Jesus.' I couldn't go to Him, and He couldn't come to me. The light emanating from Him was very powerful. And I was weeping and sweating all over, involuntarily. Jesus told me: 'Yes, I am the only One who can give you a new life—the new life you are searching for. Believe in Me, and follow Me.' He came to me three nights in a row. On the second night He told me I would get out of that place and go out into the world as His witness."

Soon after this shaking experience, the same nurse who'd given Tamrat the gospel tract gave him a Bible. That day he plowed into the Psalms. "I was reading [the Bible] day and night, continually, sometimes nonstop," he says. "I loved it, and whenever I read the Bible it would bring tears." Nevertheless, Tamrat told me his new-found faith did not sway his plans to murder the men who'd stolen his life. He was adamant about pursuing his revenge, as soon as he could find a way to get out of prison. Some months later, Layne says Jesus once again intruded into his cell to drop a boulder on his head: "I heard Jesus say in a clear voice, 'Your fate is hidden in Me; because I've forgiven you, you must forgive those who hurt you.' I spent the whole night struggling with Jesus. I was not ready right away to release the revenge and anger from my soul. I was not ready to obey Him. But He spent the whole night trying to persuade me. At the end of the night, I surrendered and repented. I knew I must begin praying for the men who'd destroyed my life and betrayed me. As I prayed, it was like a dagger coming out of my heart. I felt totally relieved—my burden just went away, and I sensed freedom." A few days later he was not only free in spirit but free in body—released from prison through the supernatural intervention of God.[2]

As both Saul and Tamrat learned, if the load is too heavy for more subtle forms of shrewd, Jesus will bring the blunt. It is one of His most effective methods of persuasion—"Let me make you an offer you can't refuse."

The Results: Albert Mohler, president of the Southern Baptist Theological Seminary, says: "Christianity, stripped of its offensive theology, is reduced to one 'spirituality' among others."[3] And Christianity is offensive in its theology because Jesus Himself is offensive—often and everywhere. He understands how things work and therefore knows that a theological debate by the campfire won't get it done with Saul. And He understands that it will take more than a polite nudge to get a former communist insurgent who fought his way to the top of the Ethiopian power pyramid to drop his plans for revenge. When the object that must be levered is heavy and immovable, shrewd bluntness is required. This is why Jesus is so theatrically offensive in most of His encounters with the Pharisees—they are immovable in their commitment to hypocritical law-keeping and will certainly perish apart from the saving grace of God unless He can get them to move.

One day a Pharisee politely asks Jesus to have lunch with him, and Jesus accepts the invitation to recline at his table. But the Pharisee, well conditioned to doggedly follow a near-ridiculous array of religious practices and ceremonial regimens, notices that Jesus has not "baptized" his hands before the meal by washing them. And so the Pharisee reacts the way you would if a chef at a restaurant had neglected to wash his hands after going to the bathroom—he was "surprised." Disgusted is probably more like it. And Jesus, the invited guest at a distinguished man's home, responds with this: "Now you Pharisees clean the outside of the cup and of the platter; but inside of you, you are full of robbery and wickedness." He goes on to call the man and his Pharisee friends "foolish" and "concealed tombs," warning them that their copious attention to the "outside of their cup" will bring many "woes" upon them. And then, a wide-eyed lawyer who thinks he's an innocent bystander to this assault offers this laugh-out-loud response: "Teacher, when You say this, You insult us too." Jesus, now aware He might have missed a target or two with one of His blunt missiles, turns his attention to the lawyers in the room, filling the air with offensive accusations (Luke 11:37–54). Is Jesus throwing a temper tantrum, or is He exercising blunt leverage on their souls? Say something diplomatic to one who is entrenched in evil, and you won't get even a raised eyebrow; but say something purposefully offensive and blunt, and you get movement. And when you get the immovable rock moving, you have a much better chance of redirecting its momentum.

The Conclusion: When Jesus knocks Saul off his donkey and bluntly asks why he is persecuting Him, He is using the right force at the right time in the right place. And, sometimes, the immovable objects in our lives need more than a nuanced plea to get moving—they need the hard lever of blunt.

The Lever of Beauty

I've heard that a common question Christians ask is, "What's more important, the message or the art?" The implied answer is supposed to be, "The message." In other words, we should compromise the art in order to get the message across more clearly. And that's what any effective propaganda does. But as a musician and artist, I don't want to make propaganda. All beauty belongs to God. If it's good and beautiful, it came from Him.
—Michael Gungor, "Making Beautiful Things"

The Story: "Now one of the Pharisees was requesting Him to dine with him, and He entered the Pharisee's house and reclined at the table. And there was a woman in the city who was a sinner; and when she learned that He was reclining at the table in the Pharisee's house, she brought an alabaster vial of perfume, and standing behind Him at His feet, weeping, she began to wet His feet with her tears, and kept wiping them with the hair of her head, and kissing His feet and anointing them with the perfume. Now when the Pharisee who had invited Him saw this, he said to himself, 'If this man were a prophet He would know who and what sort of person this woman is who is touching Him, that she is a sinner'" (Luke 7:36–39).

The Exploration: Here we witness an act of beauty so shrewd that Jesus waxes poetic about it to the shocked Pharisees, who can't comprehend why Jesus would celebrate the grateful caresses of a prostitute. In response, He tells them a story about two debtors—one who owes little to a moneylender and one who owes much. And when both are unable to pay, the moneylender forgives the debt of both. And then Jesus asks the self-righteous and comfortably non-desperate Pharisees in the room: "Which of them will love him more?" And Simon, the master of the house, replies, "I suppose the one whom he forgave more." Graciously, Jesus responds, "You have judged correctly." And then He recounts with a relish how the woman has washed His feet with her tears and wiped them with her hair and kissed them and anointed them with oil—all while standing behind Him, because it would feel presumptuous and even, perhaps, unintentionally sexual for her to do these things in front of Him. Jesus was captured and ministered to by these acts of beauty, and He responds by offering her something equally shocking to the scandalized religious leaders in the room—He forgives her sins. As far as we know, she never asks for this grace. But the leverage of beauty moves Him to give what He has to give: "For this reason I say to you, her sins, which are many, have been forgiven." He does not diminish what she has done ("her sins, which are many")—He simply recognizes what is true, that acts of beauty are also acts of faith that move God ("Your faith has saved you; go in peace") the same way they move us (Luke 7:40–50).

My wife Bev was in a six-month small group for women, led by the wife of a seminary professor. One Sunday afternoon the group took a field trip to the Denver Art Museum—their "homework" was to pay attention to beauty, then report what they felt God was speaking to them through the beauty they discovered. One woman whose beloved mother was dying a slow death from cancer was stopped in her tracks by a painting of butterflies. It captured her. And when she whispered a prayer, asking God what was going on in her soul as she stared at the painting, His still, small voice reminded her that butterflies were once caterpillars who've emerged from their "burial clothes" into a new life—one that was far more adventurous, colorful, and free. She wept, pierced to the core. Later, her mother, two days before her death, was traveling in and out of consciousness. The daughter noticed her mom blindly reaching out in front of her, plucking at something unseen in the air, over and over. When she asked her mom what she was doing, the dying woman replied, with eyes closed, "I'm grabbing the butterflies." The nurse who showed up to care for her on the last day of her life wore a butterfly on her lapel. And the day after the woman finally weighed anchor on her earthly life, the daughter took a stroll in the garden her mom loved so much—that day it was inundated with a moving carpet of butterflies.

Beauty pierces the heart and speaks to us in ways nothing else can.

The Results: Beauty can take our breath away, but more important, it can give us a taste of a world that is real but hidden behind a veil. That world is the kingdom of God as the Trinity, and all who've been adopted into that Family, truly experience it. There, it's not the cross that's beautiful (as so many of our hymns insist)—it's the person who hung on that cross who's the essence of beauty. The cross was an ugly Roman death device. The real beauty is in Jesus's submission to death, not in the way He was killed. Beauty has a way of driving us to our knees—actually, the same way Jesus drives us to our knees when we see Him as He truly is. The psalmist urges us to "taste and see that the LORD is good" (Ps. 34:8). And good is just another way of describing beauty. When we taste beauty in any form, and respond to it, shrewdness is at work because our hearts are the targets of a sneak attack.

When terrible or fearful things happen to us, we all crave the same things—relief and the revealing of beauty behind the facade of ugly. The truth is, God is not that motivated to explain these things to us, but He's highly motivated to enter into our sorrow and turn ugly into beauty. Because beauty opens us to Him and pierces us, as surely as the nails pierced the hands of our Beloved. And when we, like the grateful and broken prostitute who gave herself to Jesus, offer beauty to those around us, we often succeed in *moving* them.

Not long ago I spent a lot of time with a tough ex-cop from Baltimore. I was speaking at a Youth for Christ event in Maryland, and the guy assigned to ferry me around was Rob Benson, a former street cop who left all that to fuel his passion for reaching teenagers for Christ. As Rob drove me in his van from the airport to the venue to the hotel and back again, I asked lots of questions—he fascinated me. Rob has a heart for the no-hopers—kids who scare or intimidate or depress the other adults in their lives. His ministry is essentially a lost-and-found outpost for teenagers who've slipped through the cracks. Sitting just behind me in the van—always—was a senior high boy who was born in one of the breakaway Soviet Bloc countries. He'd been adopted by an American family in Rob's church.

Whenever there was a lull in the conversation, I asked this young guy about his life. The stories started out slightly over-the-top and quickly progressed to unbelievable and bizarre—midnight escapes from the Russian Mafia, cross-border treks to freedom, and so on. It dawned on me that this guy was either delusional or the lost son of James Bond. He was always with Rob during the event, staying with him in his hotel room, riding with him to run errands, and helping him at the conference. Early on, Rob could see my mental gears grinding and pulled me aside. He told me that this kid had some mental issues—he'd indeed been adopted by an American family, but his outbursts, delusional ramblings, and sometimes scary behavior meant the family had been forced to find a special group home for him. Meanwhile, Rob had latched on to him, picking him up for every ministry gathering and taking him to conferences like the one we were at.

It brings tears to my eyes right now as I write about this. Rob, in the deepest sense, was using the leverage of beauty to rescue this lost and delusional kid—he was moving toward this "lost sheep" with the reckless passion of Jesus, who was the first to show us the beauty of leaving the ninety-nine behind to pursue the one who's wandered away into the darkness. The other day I was watching a Sara Groves concert on DVD. In between songs, she told about a season of great fear in her life and how a friend's story released her into freedom. It was the story of a musician's unique act of protest during the early days of the Bosnian conflict. He took his cello to a bomb crater, then played his favorite piece of music while the war raged around him. Groves said she could relate to his "protest of beauty." Then she added: "This is the very protest of God—that He sent Christ in the middle of our broken darkness. He sends light and beauty. I can't think of anything more beautiful than Jesus Christ Himself. He was a protest of beauty."[1] And the beauty of this story released Groves from the fear that had gripped her, plunging her into the freedom she craved. When we offer beauty in response to death and fear and harm, we leverage others toward freedom—it's our way of crowding into the bomb crater with that cellist.

The Conclusion: Writing in "What I Understood," poet Katha Pollitt offers this reflection on the mysterious leveraging power of beauty: "[In a world of] futility, cruelty, loneliness, and disappointment / people are saved every day / by a sparrow, a foghorn, a grassblade, a tablecloth."[2] A random act of beauty draws out an eternal gift of beauty from Jesus. The metaphoric beauty of a butterfly invades a woman's grief and offers her the sweet fragrance of life in "another country." The "leave the ninety-nine" beauty of a former cop gives a delusional and difficult boy the chance to taste redemption. The everyday beauty that surrounds us has an immersing and redemptive ability to lever the hard things we suffer, like rolling a stone away from our tomb. And Jesus offers Himself as a sacrifice of beauty, the greatest leverage of all.

The Lever of Pursuit

How many of you were looking for God when you got
saved? You didn't choose God. He chose us.
—Dick Witherow, pastor of a "modern-day leper colony" in
Florida that's entirely made up of convicted sex offenders

The Story: "A man was there [the pool of Bethesda] who had been ill for thirty-eight years. When Jesus saw him lying there, and knew that he had already been a long time in that condition, He said to him, 'Do you wish to get well?'" (John 5:5–6).

The Exploration: As I've explored earlier in this book, Jesus used questions like a shepherd's crook—reaching out with them to snag His wandering sheep. And in this encounter, He knows this hobbled man has been coming to the "healing pool" near Jerusalem's sheep gate for almost four decades, so He quickly assesses "how things work" with him, then asks the one question no one else in his life has likely ever asked him. It's a question fueled by artful pursuit, and it does the trick. Instead of scorning Jesus because He's asked an obvious question, the man publicly affirms his hunger for healing and meekly offers an explanation for why he's been coming to the pool for so long, with no good result. In effect, he tells Jesus that he wants healing, but needs help. And so Jesus reaches out with His question-crook and drags the man's desperate dependence and faith out of hiding—the man must respond to His pursuit before Jesus will "give what He has to give." Again, just as the engineers studied the paths in the grass before they laid down the concrete, the shrewd purpose of Jesus's pursuit is to understand how we work so that He can pry open our complacency and move us to get engaged in our own rescue.

A while back a friend of mine wrote to ask for help in pursuing the heart of a young foster-care girl whom she'd recently committed to mentoring. Her normal, "frontal" approach to engaging this girl in conversation was failing—their times together were dominated by awkward silences. Here's what she wrote:

> I recently starting mentoring a sixteen-year-old girl.
> She is really quiet, really sweet. We have done some
> "activities" together—group volleyball, took her to
> Extreme Community Makeover on Saturday, and so
> on. But when I have just taken her out for ice cream
> or a picnic, there have been some quiet moments.
> I know her "file"—she's living in a foster home and
> her foster mother is trying to adopt her and they
> have a good relationship. The foster mom has shared
> some with me too. [The girl has] been in foster care

since she was nine, and in this home for three years.
I know some about her biological parents—she's not
seen two younger siblings since she was nine. She has
never talked about any of this to me (I just know all
of this from her file or her foster mom). Nor have
I asked her about it; she's young, she doesn't know
me. She sees a therapist; it's all pretty heavy, and I'm
not a therapist! She refers to her foster mom as "my
mom." I guess I'm looking for some "safe" but nevertheless thought-provoking, somewhat probing topics
to discuss. I was hoping you might have guidance
for me as I go into these unchartered, out-of-my-
comfort-zone waters![1]

My response to my friend centered around a three-filter strategy I
use to train folks in a more proactive, penetrating, and unlocking way
to pursue people. It's a shrewd approach to "can-opening" people—
one that Jesus used over and over. The three question-filters are:

1. Surprising: the person doesn't see the question
   coming.
2. Specific: it's a question about one specific thing—
   not multiple issues.
3. Personal: it asks for a personal—not a general,
   rhetorical, or theoretical—response.

So I sent my friend a few examples of the kind of questions I was
suggesting, crafted with this girl in mind:

- Some people would love to win the lottery because they think that would solve all their problems— what do you think would "solve all your problems"? Why?
- What's something about yourself that you secretly admire, and why?
- What qualities are common threads that run through your friends? Why are you drawn to the friends you have?
- When you're really troubled or worried, what helps you feel at peace again? Explain why that's true for you.

Like riding a bike for the first time, when we're first learning to pursue people like Jesus does, we tend to overthink the "formula" and stumble around. But the more we do it, the more we can stop overthinking our questions and have fun with them. Once you learn how to "ride this bike," it will take you to places faster than you've ever been able to get to them on foot—I mean, you will lever open authentic places in the lives of your friends, enemies, and the person you're standing behind in the grocery checkout line. Here's Jesus teaching His disciples about the leveraging power of pursuit:

> Suppose you went to a friend's house at midnight,
> wanting to borrow three loaves of bread. You say to
> him, "A friend of mine has just arrived for a visit,
> and I have nothing for him to eat." And suppose he
> calls out from his bedroom, "Don't bother me. The

door is locked for the night, and my family and I
are all in bed. I can't help you." But I tell you this—
though he won't do it for friendship's sake, if you
keep knocking long enough, he will get up and give
you whatever you need because of your shameless
persistence. (Luke 11:5–8 NLT)

"Shameless persistence" is shrewd because it is forceful. And
"shamelessly persistent" questions act as a kind of virus that we can't
get out of our heads. A decade ago, I heard the best "viral" question
I've ever pondered—asked by a man I never knew in a place I'd never
been, surrounded by people I'd never met. And the man who asked
the question had just died in a plane crash. Let me explain….

My wife and I had a close friendship with a couple we met in a
birthing class as we prepared for our first daughter to come barrel-
ing into our world. Peter and Donna were kindred spirits in almost
every way but one—they didn't share our faith in Christ. For years
I'd heard stories about Donna's globetrotting, swashbuckling father,
Leo. He'd made and lost his fortune several times over, climbed
fourteen-thousand-foot peaks on the sunset side of his seventies, and
piloted his own Cessna for more than a quarter-century. He married
his sweetheart when he was twenty-five and stayed married to her for
fifty-one years until his death. He parented three strong, successful
children. In so many ways, Leo was unlike any man I'd ever heard
of—he loved to talk about faith in God and frequently pursued
religious conversations with people he'd just met, but he claimed he
was a staunch atheist. He was a man full of passionate opinions on
politics, social issues, economics, and world history, but time after

time Donna and Peter told us he was also a passionate listener. This man was an overshadowing force in the lives of those who knew him—the kind of man who leaves a wake of impact behind him, who lives his life with such vigor that death seems an impossibility.

But it all ended on a lonely, chilly Colorado hillside in late October. Leo was preparing to update his pilot's license by flying his Cessna at night, navigating only by the plane's instruments, in the foothills near Denver. He smashed his plane into the side of a mountain that night and died instantly. The next day, Donna called to tell us the news—she was shaken to her core, and we wept with her. Later she called again to invite us to a gathering at her parents' mountain home—an informal ceremony to honor Leo's life. We got there just as Leo's family and friends were assembling to honor him with speeches, stories, and poems. We listened as his three children, their spouses, and his former coworkers described his impact on their lives—like a boulder thrown into a still pond. The last person to speak was a young man who seemed somehow out of place in the lineup of speakers. He said: "I met Leo when I was eighteen—I think that was the best age to meet him, when I was young. A few minutes after I was first introduced to him, he looked me square in the eye and asked, 'What do you stand for?' I didn't even know I was supposed to be thinking of questions like that. But that question has dominated my life ever since."[2]

The question stunned me—I could see myself in that young man's shoes. Could I have stared back into Leo's steely eyes and answered well? On our way back home, my wife and I were discussing the question when she asked, "Rick, what do you stand for?" Almost too quickly, I replied, "I stand for the glory and honor of Jesus Christ."

In that moment, Leo's "shamelessly persistent" question wheedled its way into my heart—I think about it almost every day. It reminds me, again, of what Jesus said at the end of the Parable of the Shrewd Manager: "The people of this world are more shrewd in dealing with their own kind than are the people of the light" (Luke 16:8 NIV). Leo's question is an Alpha and Omega practice—the first and last thing to think about every day. It has helped me remember who I am and what I'm about. And it has shrewdly leveraged a greater freedom in me—pursuit at its finest.

The Results: The man who dragged himself to the edge of the Bethesda pool for most of his life was hampered in his quest for healing by his own passivity—I mean, he had acclimated himself to his condition for so long that he had made peace with it. Jesus's ridiculous question was intended to lever the man out of his learned passivity, forcing him to own his longings rather than waiting for a miracle to drop out of the sky. We need Jesus to use the lever of pursuit in our lives because our gravitational pull is toward passivity. Remember, He compares us to sheep—the same animal that lies down in a rainstorm and then can't stand to its feet because its wool is soaked with water. Without a shepherd to pursue it, the sheep's penchant for passivity will spell its doom.

A year ago I heard a report about the Czech Republic's slow progression toward democracy after decades of communist rule. One segment of the report stuck out to me—I couldn't stop thinking about it. When I got to work I found an online transcript of the conversation between reporter Eric Westervelt and Jiri Pehe, a Czech political commentator:

Westervelt: After the Velvet Revolution, the European Union and the U.S. helped the Czech Republic quickly install the machinery, the institutional structures, of democracy. But some Czechs lament that the state-will-solve-it mentality is still prevalent....

Pehe: Well, I think that twenty years after the fall of communism, we realize there is a big difference between democracy as a set of institutions—a sort of procedural democracy—and democracy understood as culture.

Westervelt: Pehe says it's proved far harder and taken longer than he'd hoped to get citizens more engaged in the deeper responsibilities of democratic citizenship, to energize people who, for forty years, were used to being only inactive, passive citizens.[3]

The result of Jesus's shrewd pursuit of us is that we move from inactivity and passivity to mission and purpose in our lives.

The Conclusion: As a people, we are locked up in captivity. Paul eloquently describes our longing for freedom in his letter to the Christians living in Rome: "For we know that the whole creation groans and suffers the pains of childbirth together until now. And not only this, but also we ourselves, having the first fruits of the Spirit, even we ourselves groan within ourselves, waiting eagerly for our adoption as sons, the redemption of our body" (Rom. 8:22–23). The "pain of childbirth" we experience is our longing for the born-again life—possible only because of His shrewd pursuit of us in the first place—"We love, because He first loved us" (1 John 4:19).

The Lever of Laughter

Some words are inherently funny. The reason does not matter. What matters is being able to identify opportunities where you can apply the principle—"Underpants Is Twenty Percent Funnier than Underwear"—and swap out boring words with funny ones.
—Brandon Mendelson, a blogger who "uses social publishing tools to inspire activism and help those in need," in a post he titled "How to Be 20% Funnier Than You Really Are"

The Story: "When it was evening, the disciples came to Him and said, 'This place is desolate and the hour is already late; so send the crowds away, that they may go into the villages and buy food for themselves.' But Jesus said to them, 'They do not need to go away; you give them something to eat!'" (Matt. 14:15–16).

The Exploration: In my Jesus-Centered Ministry experience I ask people to study some of the things Jesus said through a radical new filter—I have them assume He spoke His words while laughing. For example, reread the little story from Matthew 14 above as if Jesus was chuckling when He said, "You give them something to eat!" We almost never consider the possibility that Jesus intended some of the things He said to be both intentional *and* funny. We're not crossing a boundary here—we've already assumed the emotional context for many of His statements, and some of our assumptions are likely wrong. But you'd be surprised how many people find my "imagine Jesus laughing" exercise, at least initially, patently offensive. We're so conditioned to read the Bible, and especially the "red type" sections where Jesus is speaking, as if He were a mortician or an actuary or Ben Stein in *Ferris Bueller's Day Off.* Scripture translated from ancient Greek and Hebrew often seems stripped down to its bare essentials—that's why Eugene Peterson's paraphrase of the Bible, *The Message,* is so refreshing. Humor that has been excised from the original text, or never wholly reflected in the first place, is given a fairer hearing by Peterson. For example, when Jesus asks the Samaritan "woman at the well" in John 4 to go get her husband and bring him to the well, she tells Him, "I have no husband." And in Peterson's paraphrase, Jesus says: "That's nicely put: 'I have no husband.' You've had five husbands, and the man you're living with now isn't even your husband. You spoke the truth there, sure enough" (vv. 17–18). Here, there is laughter lurking in Jesus's response....

There are examples of Jesus's humor scattered throughout the Gospels, but because we've learned to read the Bible in a stiffly reverent way, without imagination, we "hear" these stories in our head as all serious. I know that using the word *imagination* in reference to reading the Bible sounds suspect on the face of it. But whether or not we admit it, we're using our imagination by default every time we read anything—that's the fundamental way we translate words on a page to pictures in our head. The Bible gives very little information about the emotional "delivery" of the things Jesus said. For example, it's not a given that Jesus spoke to "Doubting Thomas" in a stern, confrontational way when He said, after He suddenly appeared to the disciples in a locked room after His resurrection, "Put your finger here; see my hands. Reach out your hand and put it into my side. Stop doubting and believe" (John 20:27 NIV). I think it's just as likely that Jesus said this with a smile on His face, even laughing when He said it. Can you imagine yourself sitting next to the resurrected Jesus, eating a meal—and not having a goofy smile on your face, and seeing one on His? I can't…. But we're so conditioned to see Jesus as intense and serious, we just assume everything He said was grave.

In so many ways humor is a mystery to us—why do I laugh at subtly satirical things while my wife scrunches her forehead and narrows her eyes? Why am I so wholeheartedly amused when I'm making caustic fun of our cats while Bev frowns and winces? And why does she have a strange and sometimes disturbing addiction to slapstick when I can't bear it? Though it's a mystery, the power of laughter to open us to greater intimacy is unrivaled. When Bev and I first came to Greenwood Community Church in Denver we were tired, so tired, of our vagabond church history. Even though our past was marked by long-term commitments to church bodies, we'd somehow gotten ourselves banished to the wilderness, wandering from church to church, trying to plant our roots but not succeeding. The day we walked through the door at Greenwood we were in the ugly middle of Bev's second bed-bound pregnancy—because of an immune-system disorder, Bev's body decoded the baby in her womb, our daughter Emma, as a threat, and did everything possible to expulse the enemy invader. That translated to misery for Bev, who spent day after day in a darkened room, flat on her back, where even the motion of the TV screen could bring on unendurable nausea.

So on this day, remarkably, she felt well enough to get out of bed and drag herself to church with our four-year-old daughter, Lucy. We crept into the sanctuary and sat down at a visitor-safe distance, two-thirds of the way back, on the side. When the pastor, Tom Melton, stepped to the podium for his sermon I thought he looked entirely ordinary. But when he opened his mouth I was struck by how relaxed he was, like he was chatting with us in his living room. And a couple of minutes into his sermon he said something off-the-cuff that was funny—*and the entire congregation exploded in laughter.* It startled me, to tell the truth. It was the laughter of a family that delights in each other, the laughter of people who feel safe with each other, and the laughter of an environment saturated in trust. You can't laugh, really laugh from your core, around people you don't trust. And that kind of trust happens when people know they're among others who, like them, are broken and redeemed and unashamed by the love of Jesus. I knew in that moment that we had finally found our home— any church body that could laugh the way this one laughed must have found its way through the brambles toward intimacy with Jesus and one another.

And our first impression was just the tip of the iceberg—the closer we got to the people in the "engine room" of the church, the better we experienced them. Founded and staffed by veterans of the Christian parachurch ministry Young Life, a youth ministry move-ment that strategically uses humor as its primary "net," Greenwood has laughter embedded in its DNA. One highlight every year is a twenty-year tradition called Club Valentino—it's sort of a version of *The Carol Burnett Show* (a succession of skits buffered by musical performances) for the church, put on by staff and elders and their spouses. Our second year in the church, we decided to check out what this dinner-variety-show thing was all about and were stunned to discover that we had to enter a *lottery* for tickets—all four nights typically sell out. The night of the performance, we walked into a church building that had been totally transformed by over-the-top sets and decorations throughout. In the sanctuary we found our seats at a table with three other couples and then, for the next three hours, laughed our heads off as the staff and elders at the church performed skits stolen from Young Life and Tim Conway and the old *Sid Caesar Show* and *Mr. Bean* and *Saturday Night Live*.

Throughout the evening we heard no mention of God except for the opening welcome and brief prayer over the meal. And I really loved that—laughter was not an "appetizer" for the more serious pursuits of the Christian life; it was the main course. As we got up to find our car and drive home, our faces hurt from laughing so long and so hard. Afterward, we felt remarkably bonded to the staff and congregation, and something in us was significantly more relaxed and open to sharing our lives. Now, as an elder for the last four years, I've been on stage instead of in the audience. From both perspectives, I think Club Valentino is one of the most subversively shrewd ministry ideas I've ever seen. People who typically maintain a guarded distance at church see their walls breached, and the palpable atmosphere of enjoying one another has a healing power in their lives. Also, church leaders are forced out of their comfort zones in a supportive, energizing, and sometimes-intense creative community. For many who now attend the church regularly, Club Valentino is the "welcome mat" for entry into a commitment to following Jesus, but not because they are intentionally funneled that way. Club Valentino is the very definition of obliquity—moving sideways instead of frontally.

Now, a decade in to our adoption into this family, we have been profoundly changed by the laughter that is the lifeblood of this church. It's no stretch to say that God has used laughter to heal us, invite us, expose us, and draw us to Him. And that's exactly why laughter is perhaps the most surprising of all conduits for shrewdness—it can move us when little else will.

The Results: No, the Bible doesn't give a lot of emotional context for the things Jesus said and did—it also excises everyday activities like going to the bathroom or getting dressed in the morning or sneezing or tripping over something or taking a bath. But we know, because He's both God and man, that Jesus did these things. And for the same reason, we know He laughed His head off at times, just like other human beings. People were magnetically drawn to Jesus, and we're typically not drawn to people who are dour or who suck the energy out of the room when they walk in. The children who were always coming up to Jesus would never gravitate to an adult who comes off like Ebenezer Scrooge, or one who's so distracted by His "mission" that He doesn't notice them or invite them through His words and body language. Jesus was an electric person, more alive than anyone you or I know. And the most alive people in my life know how to laugh, usually with the sort of abandon that freedom allows.

Have you ever met anyone who's deeply secure in the love of their parents who does not laugh easily and often? I haven't…. And no one in history was more secure in the love of His Father than Jesus. In *A Long Obedience in the Same Direction*, Eugene Peterson says that the Hebrew root word for "prosperity" is more accurately translated "leisure"—"the relaxed stance of one who knows that everything is all right because God is over us, with us and for us in Jesus Christ."[1] That has stuck with me—those who share in the life of God *live* in prosperity, or are utterly relaxed in themselves. They naturally use humor to offer a kind of saturating hope to others.

Pain is a predator, and all of us have felt its bite—some have been eaten alive by it. But laughter raises its fist to a corrupted world and proclaims, "This cannot destroy me!" This is, in the end, the message delivered in the 1997 Oscar-winning foreign film *Life Is Beautiful*. In the film a Jewish-Italian man named Guido (played by writer/director/actor Roberto Benigni) uses laughter to help his four-year-old son survive a Nazi concentration camp. He convinces his son that the camp is just an elaborate game, and that the boy will win an actual tank if he's the first child to earn one thousand points. He will lose points, explains Guido, if he cries, complains about missing his mother, or begs for food. Despite his stark and horrific surroundings, the boy believes his dad's version of reality—the killing factory becomes his playground. In the end, as American liberators are closing in on the camp, Guido is caught trying to find his wife and led off by Nazi guards to be shot. He sees his son watching as he's taken away, so he mimics and satirizes the guard as he marches behind him, to the delight of his son. The father is killed, but the son and the mother survive. Later, when the boy is old enough to understand what happened, he realizes that his father's shrewd sense of humor saved his life.

When we have the courage to laugh in the midst of struggle and pain, we're affirming that our hope in God survives. I think that's why the apostle Paul says, "We are afflicted in every way, but not crushed; perplexed, but not despairing; persecuted, but not forsaken; struck down, but not destroyed" (2 Cor. 4:8–9). Laughter is the "but not" of the Christian life. And shrewdness, as we know, always meets us where we are and does something to change our trajectory. The other day my youth pastor friend Jonathan Kelly emailed me this: "If you need a laugh today, I was correcting some Bible quizzes for the middle school classes I teach—the students had to list the six parts of the armor of God from Ephesians. Here was one response: 'Belt of truth, sword of the Spirit, helmet of salvation, shoes of the gospel of peace, body armor of righteousness, and glove of the King of Pop.' I'm tempted to give him credit just for originality."[2] In the middle of my laughter, I'm paying attention, in a new way, to the armor I wear and the hope I have. This is why laughter is such a subversive and leveraging weapon in the kingdom of God.

The Conclusion: Political commentator Ed Rollins says, "Humor with some truth in it is always dangerous."[3] Those like Jesus who wield the lever of laughter most effectively use it as a defense-dropper—while we're laughing, they're jumping over our lowered walls to plant a little truth in our garden. This is why the award-winning *Dilbert* cartoon strip has transcended the genre, often wielding more influence on the business community than best-selling business books—creator Scott Adams delivers a payload of business wisdom using the "launch vehicle" of laughter. Media analyst Norman Solomon points to the way executives at Xerox have used characters and dialogue from *Dilbert* in a series of internal pamphlets designed to obliquely plant the seeds of corporate culture in its managers. "Xerox management had recognized what more gullible *Dilbert* readers did not," says Solomon. "*Dilbert* is an offbeat sugary substance that helps the corporate medicine go down. The *Dilbert* phenomenon accepts—and perversely eggs on—many negative aspects of corporate existence as unchangeable facets of human nature.... As Xerox managers grasped, *Dilbert* speaks to some very real work experiences while simultaneously eroding inclinations to fight for better working conditions."[4]

Humor is a context changer, moving us from caution to openness to intimacy. We're such guarded, well-defended people—and humor has an amazing ability to punch holes in our walls. This is why shrewdly innocent people know how to "help the medicine go down" with laughter.

The Lever of Generosity

*Keep going. Don't quit, son. Keep
playing. Don't stop. Don't quit.*
—What the world-famous Polish pianist Ignacy Jan
Paderewski supposedly said to a young boy who sneaked
onto an empty stage just before his sold-out concert
performance and started playing "Chopsticks"—the angry
crowd tried to shout the boy off the stage, but legend
has it that Paderewski rushed to his side and played
harmony with him through the end of the song.

The Story: "One of the criminals hanging alongside cursed him: 'Some Messiah you are! Save yourself! Save us!' But the other one made him shut up: 'Have you no fear of God? You're getting the same as him. We deserve this, but not him—he did nothing to deserve this.' Then he said, 'Jesus, remember me when you enter your kingdom.' He said, 'Don't worry, I will. Today you will join me in paradise'" (Luke 23:39–43 MSG).

The Exploration: When you're dying, it's not an easy thing to treat others with generosity—and when you've been crucified, mocked, scourged, taunted, and abandoned, generosity is unthinkable. But Jesus was generous to the thief on the cross because generosity is fundamental to His nature. Generosity, like laughter, is a powerful way to lever open closed, bolted, and barricaded doors in a person's soul. His generous response to the thief on the cross did not demand an explanation for his past behavior or even an overt act of repentance. Jesus gave, because Jesus gives. And when we offer unexpected generosity the way Jesus offers it, we're using shrewd leverage the way He uses it.

For three weeks I had two college-age guys working in my backyard, scraping and painting our decrepit-looking deck. I know, because I was doing that kind of work when I was their age, that people tend to treat laborers as faceless cogs, a paid-for means to an end. And I knew from experience that people who treated me generously made me want to work harder and do a better job. The surprise inherent in generosity is leveraging—it always *moves* me when I experience it. So, on their first day on the job, I erected an umbrella near where they were working so they could take a break in the shade, and served them a couple of big glasses of ice water that I refilled throughout the day—an almost insignificant act of generosity that *really* mattered to these guys. It was a little thing that leveraged a big thing—they worked hard and did a good job because, in part, a little generosity had obliterated the master-slave vibe that had initially framed our relationship. We became people to each other. I got a window into the lives of two guys who are working their way through school; they got treated with respect and curiosity and sensitivity. And we all got the satisfaction of a job well done. I'm generous not because I'm trying to manipulate people to do what I want them to do—I'm generous because it's a fruit of the Spirit, and the Spirit is always finding ways to *move* us.

Generosity is shrewd because it has the power to pry open the heavy armor people wear to sheath their hearts. That's one of the profound truths locked up in one of my favorite films—Bille August's 1998 version of *Les Miserables*, based on a story written by Victor Hugo more than two hundred years ago. The film follows the story of ex-convict Jean Valjean, a man in pre-revolutionary France who was imprisoned for nineteen years of hard labor after he stole a loaf of bread for his hungry family. Valjean is released from prison, but because he's an ex-convict he can't get a job. He is bitter and hardened and as distrustful as a dog that's been repeatedly beaten. He resorts to stealing valuable silverware from a kind bishop who invites him into his home—Valjean injures the bishop and escapes when he's caught in the act. But he is captured by the French police and dragged back to the bishop's home with the loot in his bag. In a powerful scene, the bishop shrewdly keeps Valjean from going to jail—literally, he uses his cunning to redeem him, and he challenges Valjean to live his life for God.

From this point on Valjean lives passionately for God and for the poor and oppressed. He becomes a successful businessman and political leader. When one of his workers is wrongfully fired from his factory (without Valjean's knowledge), she descends into poverty and prostitution and bitterness toward Valjean, who she believes ordered her firing. The woman, Fantine, struggles to stay alive on the street as she sends what little money she makes to the (wicked, it turns out) Thénardiers, who are taking care of her daughter, Cosette. By the time Valjean realizes what has happened to Fantine, and how he unknowingly played a part in it, the woman is ravaged by consumption and has endured terrible abuse. So, in an act of courageous generosity, he takes Fantine into his home, where he blows on the embers of her dead heart, trying to bring it back to life. In this excerpt from the script, Fantine lies in bed while Valjean cares for her, striving to bring her raging fever down by wiping her face with a cool wet cloth:

> **Fantine:** But I don't understand why you're being so kind.

> **Valjean:** I was preoccupied. I didn't know. If you'd come straight to me, none of this … You need to rest.

> **Fantine:** *(Confused)* You don't want a kiss?

> **Valjean:** *(Gently)* I want you to rest. And don't worry. I'll bring your daughter to you.

> **Fantine:** You're going to the Thénardiers?

> **Valjean:** No. I can't. I'll send the money to bring Cosette here.

> **Fantine:** She can't live with me.

Valjean: Of course she can. She will. She'll attend the school, and you won't have any more worries. When you're better I'll find work for you.

Fantine: But you don't understand. I'm a whore, and Cosette has no father.

Valjean: She has the Lord. He is her Father. And you are His creation. In His eyes you have never been anything but an innocent and beautiful woman. You look better every day.

Fantine: *(Smiling)* Liar.[1]

Valjean's extravagant gift of generosity launches a redemptive relationship that softens Fantine's heart and opens her to the grace of God. He shows her his generous heart, over and over. He never pushes himself on her, never expects or requires love in return, but slowly, over time, generosity wins her trust. For some, this flavor of shrewd is the only possible way to leverage a heart long steeled against entry because of dehumanizing abuse. It is exactly how God tenderly cares for our own abused hearts—we know this for certain because we see how Jesus cares for the desperate and downtrodden who come to Him. Generosity surprises us, just as Jesus surprises the woman at the well by inviting her to drink from Him and never thirst again. We're all thirsty for generosity—that's why it's often the shrewdest way to melt a cold or closed or hurting heart.

The Results: So, why did one of the great American singers of all time, Frank Sinatra, choose an obscure Italian restaurant in New York City as his favorite hangout, ignoring a host of swankier, better-located options? Many forget that Sinatra, a legendary performer, suffered through years of embarrassing failure in the early '50s, when his career was crashing. During that season of shame, the owner of Patsy's on West 56th Street, Pasquale "Patsy" Scognamillo, used to sit with Sinatra as he ate his lunch, alone and shunned by the people he called "my fair-weather friends." One year, on the eve of Thanksgiving, Sinatra quietly made a reservation with Patsy to eat alone the next day, asking him to serve "anything but turkey." Sinatra wanted to forget that he had nowhere to go on Thanksgiving, but he didn't want to be alone. The restaurant was supposed to be closed on Thanksgiving, but Patsy didn't tell Sinatra that. He invited the families of the restaurant's staff to come in for dinner, too, so the singer wouldn't suspect what Patsy had done. Many years later, Sinatra discovered Patsy's quiet act of generosity toward him—and that's why he never stopped coming to the restaurant, even when he worked his way back to the top of the entertainment world. Many wondered about Sinatra's perplexing loyalty to Patsy's over the years, but Pulitzer Prize-winning columnist Bob Greene says: "It was no big secret to the Scognamillo family. They all knew. A person recalls how he is treated not when he is on top of the world, undefeated, but when he is at his lowest, thinking he will never again see the sun."[2] And when the thief asks Jesus to remember him in Paradise, and Jesus responds with shocking generosity, what happens in the thief's heart? Likely, this man who was haunted by his guilt and shame is even now "recalling how he was treated not when he was on top of the world … but when he was at his lowest" as he enjoys the "pearl of great price" in the kingdom of God.

The Conclusion: In a story that has found its way all over the Internet, nurse JoAnn C. Jones remembers a tipping-point moment in her path toward a career in the medical world:

> During my second year of nursing school our profes-
> sor gave us a quiz. I breezed through the questions
> until I read the last one: "What is the first name
> of the woman who cleans the school?" Surely this
> was a joke. I had seen the cleaning woman several
> times, but how would I know her name? I handed
> in my paper, leaving the last question blank. Before
> the class ended, one student asked if the last ques-
> tion would count toward our grade. "Absolutely,"
> the professor said. "In your careers, you will meet
> many people. All are significant. They deserve your
> attention and care, even if all you do is smile and say
> hello." I've never forgotten that lesson. I also learned
> her name was Dorothy.[3]

We know how the professor's challenge changed JoAnn Jones, but we don't know how his lesson on living generously ultimately impacted Dorothy, the cleaning lady. If Jesus's example of shrewd generosity is a template, it might have saved Dorothy's life.

Astonish Me

....

A Benediction

The center of attraction in a true church is the Lord Jesus Christ.
—A. W. Tozer, *Tozer on Worship and Entertainment*

Look for Christ and you will find Him, and
with Him everything else thrown in.
—C. S. Lewis, *Mere Christianity*

Or suppose a king is about to go to war against another king. Will he
not first sit down and consider whether he is able with ten thousand
men to oppose the one coming against him with twenty thousand?
—Jesus in Luke 14:31 (NIV)

He's a professional soldier—battle-hardened and tough as nails. He leads eighty "legionaries" who are sworn to protect Rome. His rank is centurion, which places him among an elite fraternity of men who've distinguished themselves by out-soldiering their contemporaries. Like the men he commands, he must be able to march twenty miles a day in full armor while carrying his own shield, a weapon, some food, and camping equipment. He must be, according to the Roman definition, a man who is "brave, clever, and fights well."[1] But on this day the warrior is not fighting the enemies of Rome—he's come hat in hand to ask a young Jewish rabbi, a religious leader from the occupied territory, for help. This alone is remarkable, but the unthinkable is about to be overshadowed by the unbelievable. Today he has humbled himself not because of his own desperate need, but because his "servant lies at home paralyzed and in terrible suffering" (Matt. 8:6 NIV). So the humble centurion, driven by love for a trusted friend, formally asks Jesus to heal his suffering servant. And Jesus, conventionally, offers to go to the man's home. And that's when the impossible happens—*Jesus is taken off guard by the man's shrewdness*:

> The centurion replied, "Lord, I do not deserve to
> have you come under my roof. But just say the word,
> and my servant will be healed. For I myself am a
> man under authority, with soldiers under me. I tell
> this one, 'Go,' and he goes; and that one, 'Come,'
> and he comes. I say to my servant, 'Do this,' and he
> does it."
>
> When Jesus heard this, he was astonished and
> said to those following him, "I tell you the truth,
> I have not found anyone in Israel with such great
> faith. I say to you that many will come from the

east and the west, and will take their places at the
feast with Abraham, Isaac and Jacob in the kingdom
of heaven. But the subjects of the kingdom will be
thrown outside, into the darkness, where there will
be weeping and gnashing of teeth."

Then Jesus said to the centurion, "Go! It will be
done just as you believed it would." And his servant
was healed at that very hour. (vv. 8–13 NIV)

How'd you like to be the one who "astonishes" Jesus? How is it
even *possible* to astonish Him? Surprise is fundamental to shrewdness because surprise translates to leverage. This is truly a man in
full—an adult in every sense. He first honors Jesus ("I do not deserve
to have you come under my roof"), and then he shrewdly *moves*
Jesus. Because he understands how things work (Jesus has authority
over sickness and disease), he knows that a word from Jesus (the
right force at the right time in the right place) is all that's required.
So, simply, that's what he asks for. All true adults are fundamentally childlike, and like a child, the centurion is not tentative in his
request—children ask for *way* too much because they haven't yet
learned to hedge their bets. The other day, after my eight-year-old
daughter Emma heard about a friend's vacation to Hawaii, she asked
when exactly we would be going to Hawaii. I told her some version of *not anytime soon, dear—that's an expensive vacation.* And she
looked at me with shock and asked, "But why not?" Like Emma, the
centurion has no problem asking way too much of Jesus because he's
fully convinced He can deliver. Metaphorically, he's shoving all his
chips into the center of the table and "calling." He bets it all on what

he believes about Jesus. This same algorithm repeats itself in every encounter that "astonishes" Jesus, including the men who go all-in in their belief about Jesus by digging a hole in the roof of a home so they can lower their paralytic friend through it to be healed (Mark 2:3–5).

There are aspects of shrewd living that only people who are determined to go all-in with Jesus truly understand. Like the centurion, people who live under authority and exercise authority understand that faith is not about believing hard enough in something until you receive it. Faith, they know, is belief in the truth about who their Captain is, and therefore a certainty about His *capabilities*. It's crucial for us to learn from warriors like the centurion because, as we know, we are in a pitched battle with an Enemy who's bent on "killing, stealing, and destroying." But most of us functionally live as civilians, not as combatants, even though we've had plenty of warning about our Enemy and have heard a boatload of stories about his character, behavior, and future plans. And we have all, in one way or another and at one time or another, been played for fools by him. Why? Because he's willing to move shrewdly to accomplish his evil intent, and encounters spotty resistance from a body of Christ that is good at trying hard, minding its manners, and following principles but is often terrible at outflanking, outsmarting, and out-leveraging him. Not much has changed since Jesus first told the Parable of the Shrewd Manager—"the people of this world are more shrewd in dealing with their own kind than are the people of the light" (Luke 16:8 NIV). When we live in territory long occupied by the Enemy of God and the unseen "principalities" that we've repeatedly been told are intent on destroying us, the "weapons of our warfare" are all arrows in the quiver of shrewd. Because warriors like the centurion are fluent in the language of all-in—by definition, they have already decided to risk their lives for a cause—they are therefore well conditioned for learning the art of shrewd. And going all-in on behalf of another is maybe the best definition of love that we have.

The first time I preached at my church, filling in for Tom Melton when he was on vacation, a guy I had only just met named Ned was the fill-in worship leader. Later that week Ned and I met for coffee to debrief the experience. I asked him what he thought of my sermon— it had been very well received by the congregation, so I assumed I was lobbing a slow pitch across the plate for him to slam over the fence. I mean, Ned and I had quickly connected in a kindred way, and we had both developed a sort of delighted appreciation of the other. I assumed he would tell me how great the sermon was—how much it had moved him. And he did … sort of. He first assured me that he had really enjoyed it, but there was something in his tone that left me hanging. Subtly, he was inviting me to pursue him further. And when I did, he told me I had done something throughout my sermon that really bothered him. I leaned in, startled but unwilling to betray the sudden nervousness I felt. I wanted to be the kind of person who was fundamentally open to critique, and yet that desire could easily be trumped by my fear of failure.

Because my surface response was inviting, Ned looked me in the eye and lowered the boom: he told me he was disappointed that I had hedged my bets in the sermon by often prefacing declarative statements with "I think." Instead of simply proclaiming a truth—"Jesus is the shrewdest man who ever lived," for example—I subtly altered what I truly believed by saying, "*I think* Jesus is the shrewdest man who ever lived." A nuance, no doubt, but a profound one that both exposed something in me and forcefully nudged me to stop playing it safe and "give what I have to give" with more courageous abandon. His critique was surprising and oblique and shrewdly redemptive. I have since tried to obliterate "I think" from my spoken and written words, challenging myself to go all-in with what God has revealed to me, then letting the chips fall where they may. Had Ned been less of a warrior, refusing to offer me the force of his shrewd response in an attitude of innocence and, instead, playing it safe by simply complimenting my sermon, I would be less free and more cowardly than I am today. Shrewdness that is restrained and fueled by innocence sets people free, and that is the reason why Jesus is so insistent that we grow in it—He loves us and wants to set us free. And He is all-in about it.

In John 8, Jesus uses a shrewd warrior's instincts to save the life of a woman caught in adultery. In the middle of a tense standoff with the conniving and murderous Pharisees who have carefully set their trap for Him, He crouches to write something in the dirt. What is He doing? So many have guessed that He's writing the sins of those who were holding stones or some such other total shot in the dark. So I'll add my own shot in the dark: I think Jesus is just doodling in the dirt, simply buying Himself some time to consult with His Father and the Holy Spirit on the shrewd path forward. "Father, I'm in a tight spot here! A little help …" He is determined to bring rescue to this woman, and He needs a shrewd way to win her freedom. A brief consultation with the Spirit is necessary. In my ill-conceived ramble through the thick maze of brambles above St. Benedict's monastery, I did the same thing, often. I'd stop, look around at my options, and listen for the Spirit's leading. Then I'd move. But no lives were on the line, really. I didn't have a woman's life hanging in the balance, dependent on the next thing I said. But the truth is, there are lives hanging in the balance all around us, and our willingness to act shrewdly on their behalf is more of a life-and-death choice than we'd like to admit.

It's ironic that I feel compelled to write this book, by the way, because I've always thought of myself as prey for those who are shrewd—the quarry, not the hunter. My deficiencies when it comes to shrewdness, and the destruction that I've suffered and inflicted in my life because of them, are the catalyst for this quest in the first place. Just as George Bailey was full of fury when he realized shrewd Old Man Potter was trying to destroy him, my anger and frustration and *yearning* fueled a quest to learn a new way of living and breathing and moving. What do you do if you don't have what your Master says you *have to have*? Well, like the Samaritan woman at the well in John 4, you accept His offer of "living water" when He gives it, and you set your face to learn what it means to be shrewd, depending on the Holy Spirit, who Jesus promised would guide us into all the truth (John 16:13).

I now have a healthy skepticism for the frontal approach I've relied upon to take on every challenge, difficulty, and opportunity that crosses my way. The way that has felt so bold and authentic to me is, bluntly, *immature and useless in many situations.* My shrewdless ways have done little to advance God's kingdom in situations that call for cunning. And the Enemy of God has sometimes toyed with me like a cat toys with a mouse—specifically because I was unwilling and unable to depend on my Guide's leading and go all *Survivor* on him ("outwit, outplay, and outlast").

If I want to understand the deep heart of Jesus and the method behind all His madness, I'll have to study Him through the lens of shrewd. If I'm going to help advance the kingdom of God the way He *needs* me to do, I'll need to go sideways—out of my way and up the ridge. We, the followers of Christ, are called to spread the kingdom of God as the sons and daughters of the king ("He sent them out to preach the kingdom of God"—Luke 9:2 NIV), and that king is telling us to learn the *only* thing we can learn from the shrewd manager—to beat back evil and unearth beauty by using the levers He's given us and modeled for us. There's so much we don't understand about the way Jesus lived His life and the sometimes-incomprehensible things He told us to do. But He's asking us to follow Him as grown-ups, not toddlers. He longs for us to hunger for the "meat" He's offering and is frustrated when we settle for "milk." I don't know many true grown-ups, to be honest. But I want to be one. I bet you do too. To get there, we'll need to leave the rutted path of principle-based Christian living and, instead, plunge into the wild and follow the shrewdest man who ever lived into the greatest adventure there ever was.

What's the worst that could happen?

Well, people might feel a little more nervous around us—more dissonant and uncertain. But, in our wake, maybe they'll get a whiff of who they really are and who Jesus really is. And maybe their dissonance will nudge them to consider Jesus in a way they never have before. And maybe the wrestling match that our shrewd gift of love produces in their souls will get them moving away from the slow death of a life lived in "quiet desperation," as Thoreau described our common addiction, and toward a more dangerous life of freedom.

It's dangerous because we can, if we play our cards right, lose our life so that we find it (Matt. 10:39). And when we "find our life," the certain side effect is that Jesus *becomes* our life. And when Jesus becomes our life, there are two more certainties: the world is going to change because the kingdom of God will expand its reach on earth, and we will know Jesus, as we have been fully known (1 Cor. 13:12). To know and to be known by the Great Lover of our souls, and to be brave enough to humbly serve as a conduit for God's love in a world that knows heartbreak and destruction far better than wholeness and healing—can the sum of our lives ever add up to more than this? We love because He first loved us. And we live innocently shrewd, because He first showed us Himself.

Notes

Introduction

1. *The Young Victoria*, directed by Jean-Marc Vallée (2009; Culver City, CA: Sony Pictures, 2010), DVD.

2. This overview is referenced in Christopher Hibbert, *Queen Victoria: A Personal History* (London: HarperCollins, 2000).

3. Robert Frost, "The Road Not Taken," *The Mountain Interval* (New York: Henry Holt and Company, 1920).

4. "Tunisia to Egypt to …" *Chicago Tribune*, January 28, 2011, http://articles.chicagotribune.com/2011-01-28/news/ct-edit-arab-20110128_1_tunisia-mubarak-regime-arab-countries.

5. Information drawn from Canadian Centres for Teaching Peace, "Gene Sharp: A Biographical Profile," and from Gene Sharp, *From Dictatorship To Democracy: A Conceptual Framework For Liberation* (Boston, MA: The Albert Einstein Institution, 2002).

6. I'm indebted to my pastor and close friend Tom Melton for first offering me this definition for shrewd: "Understanding how things work."

7. Gene Sharp, interview by Steve Inskeep, "Gene Sharp, 'Clausewitz of Non-violent Warfare,' Amazed by Egypt's Youth," *Morning Edition*, February 22, 2011, NPR, www.npr.org/blogs/thetwo-way/2011/02/23/133965129/gene-sharp-clausewitz-of-nonviolent-warfare-amazed-by-egypts-youth.

8. David Macaulay, *The Way Things Work* (Boston, MA: Houghton Mifflin Company, 1988), 11.

9. A. W. Tozer, "Worship: The Missing Jewel," *Christian Publications,* 1992, 11.

10. Aik Hong Tan, interview with the author, April 11, 2011. Used with permission.

11. John Eberle, interview with the author, April 5, 2008. Used with permission.

12. P. Shipton, *The Frog and the Crocodile* (Macmillan Education, 2010).

Chapter 1: Shrewd as Serpents, Innocent as Doves

1. From the author's videotaped interviews of attendees at the annual Cross Bar X Youth Ranch Denver spaghetti dinner and silent auction, March 2008.

2. John Maxwell, "Encouragement Changes Everything," *Success Magazine,* August 2009, www.successmagazine.com/encouragement-changes-everything/PARAMS/article/761.

3. Rachel Rodriguez, "The 10-Year-Old Who Helped Apollo 11, 40 Years Later," *CNN*, July 20, 2009, http://articles.cnn.com/2009-07-20/tech/apollo11.irpt_1_apollo-antenna-grease?_s=PM:TECH.

4. Aik Hong Tan, interview with the author, April 11, 2011. Used with permission.

5. All references are from *It's a Wonderful Life*, directed by Frank Capra (1947; Paramount, 2006), DVD.

6. David Macaulay, *The Way Things Work* (Boston, MA: Houghton Mifflin Company, 1988), 11.

7. Dr. Dennis Nikitow is a two-time winner of the World Chiropractic Alliance US Chiropractor of the Year (1994 and 2008). Story used with permission.

8. Albert King, "Born Under a Bad Sign," *Born Under a Bad Sign* © 1967 Stax Records.

Chapter 2: Paths in the Grass

1. David Macaulay, *The Way Things Work* (Boston, MA: Houghton Mifflin Company, 1988), 11.

2. Joan Chittister, *Illuminated Life* (Maryknoll, NY: Orbis Books, 2000), 21.

3. Chittister, *Illuminated Life*, 22.

4. Chittister, *Illuminated Life*, 23.

5. "*The Oprah Winfrey Show* Finale," Oprah.com, May 25, 2011, http://www.oprah.com/oprahshow/The-Oprah-Winfrey-Show-Finale_1/7.

6. C. S. Lewis, *Surprised by Joy* (Orlando, FL: Harcourt, 1955), 133.

7. Lewis, *Surprised by Joy*, 134.

8. Lewis, *Surprised by Joy*, 133.

9. Chanon Ross, "Jesus Isn't Cool," *Christian Century*, September 6, 2005, http://www.christiancentury.org/article/2005-09/jesus-isn-t-cool.

10. From the episode "The Adventure of the Blue Carbuncle" on the Granada TV production of *The Adventures of Sherlock Holmes*, June 5, 1984.

11. *The Horse Whisperer*, directed by Robert Redford (Burbank, CA: Walt Disney Video, 1998), DVD.

12. Dr. Royce Frazier, lecture.

13. Bob Krulish, communication with the author, 2009. Used with permission.

14. Rachel Remen, *Kitchen Table Wisdom* (New York: Riverhead Books, 1996), 37.

15. Leonard Sweet, conversation with the author, later published in Rick Lawrence, "Second-Century Youth Ministry," *Group Magazine*, September/October 1999.

Chapter 3: Dancing the Tango

1. Emily Wurtzbacher, note to Tom Melton, April 1, 2009. Used with permission.

2. John Eldredge, *Waking the Dead* (Nashville: Thomas Nelson, 2006), 95.

3. John Kay, *Obliquity* (New York: Penguin Press, 2011), 6.

4. Oblique, by the way, is also defined as "devious" and "underhanded"—words that are kissing cousins to the word *shrewd*.

5. Seth Borenstein, "Study: It's Not Teacher, but Method that Matters," CNSnews.com, May 12, 2011, http://cnsnews.com/news/article/study-its-not-teacher-method-matters-0.

6. Kay, *Obliquity*, 71.

7. Janet Hubbard-Brown, *Scott Joplin* (New York: Chelsea House, 2006), 13–14.

8. Hubbard-Brown, *Scott Joplin*, 30.

9. Hubbard-Brown, *Scott Joplin*, 90.

10. Chris Woodstra, Gerald Brennan, and Allen Schrott, "Scott Joplin," *All Music Guide to Classical Music* (San Francisco: Backbeat Books, 2005), 667.

11. Malcolm Gladwell, *The Tipping Point* (New York: Little, Brown and Company, 2000), 105–6.

12. John Stuart Mill, *Utilitarianism*, 2nd. ed. (Indianapolis: Hackett, 2002), 3.

13. Kay, *Obliquity*, 143.

14. Mandalit Del Barco, "Los Angeles Cracks Down on Gangs, Once Again," *Morning Edition*, NPR, January 31, 2007, http://npr.org/templates/story/story.php?storyId=7090135.

15. Eric Robinson, "The Atomic Woodchuck," *Group Magazine*, May/June 1998.

16. Bono, interview by Ed Bradley, *60 Minutes,* November 20, 2005.

17. Chris Stanton, interview with the author, April 11, 2011. Used with permission.

18. Used with permission.

19. Kay, *Obliquity*, 54.

20. Oswald Chambers, *My Utmost for His Highest* (Grand Rapids: Discovery House, 1992), 162.

21. Chambers, *My Utmost for His Highest*, 177.

22. Faith Karimi, "Malawian Boy Uses Wind to Power Hope, Electrify Village," *CNN*, October 5, 2009, http://edition.cnn.com/2009/WORLD/africa/10/05/malawi.wind.boy/index.html.

23. Kim Zetter, "Teen's DIY Energy Hacking Gives African Village New Hope," *WiredScience*, October 2, 2009, http://www.wired.com/wiredscience/2009/10/kamwamba-windmill/.

24. "Biography," *William Kamkwamba*, March 22, 2012, http://williamkamkwamba.typepad.com/about.html.

25. Zetter, "Teen's DIY Energy Hacking Gives African Village New Hope," *Wired Science*.

26. Karimi, "Malawian Boy Uses Wind to Power Hope, Electrify Village," *CNN*.

27. Andrew Peterson, "Just As I Am," *Love & Thunder* © 2004 Essential Records. Used with permission.

Chapter 4: The Way of Gamaliel & The Great Knock

1. From the Mishnah, the Hebrew word translated "repetition." It's the first written recording of the Oral Law of the Jewish people. Traditionally, it is thought to have been edited around 200 CE by Rabbi Yehuda HaNasi.

2. Kyle Idleman, *Not a Fan*, (Grand Rapids: Zondervan, 2011), 120.

3. "Gamaliel's Principle," MathPages.com, July 17, 2005, http://www.mathpages.com/home/kmath431/kmath431.htm.

4. Excerpted from *Aboth di R. Nathan*, cb. xl.

5. Martin Luther, "Preface to the Epistle of St. Paul to the Romans," *Martin Luther's Basic Theological Writings*, ed. Timothy Lull (Minneapolis, MN: Augsburg Fortress, 2005), 98.

6. Lyle W. Dorsett, ed., *The Essential C. S. Lewis* (New York: Touchstone, 1996), 5.

7. C. S. Lewis, *Surprised by Joy* (Orlando, FL: Harcourt, 1955), 135–36.

8. Bruce Edwards, "*Surprised by Joy* by C. S. Lewis: A Critical Summary and Overview," June 6, 2010, http://personal.bgsu.edu/~edwards/surprised.html.

9. "What is 'positional chess'?" Chess.com, October 12, 2008, http://www.chess.com/forum/view/general/what-is-quotpositional-chessquot.

Chapter 5: The Shadow of the Snake

1. Joe Marinich, conversation with the author. Used with permission.

2. James Ryle, "The Food Fight of Faith," *Truthworks*, July 3, 2011, http://truthworks.org/?p=2308.

3. The Rolling Stones, "Sympathy for the Devil" *Beggars Banquet* © 1968 ABKCO.

4. David Petraeus, interview by Renee Montagne, "Petraeus: U.S. to Pursue 'More Nuanced' Operations In Kandahar," *Morning Edition*, NPR,

September 15, 2010, http://www.npr.org/blogs/thetwo-way/2010/09
/14/129857868/petraeus-u-s-to-pursue-more-nuanced-operations-in
-kandahar.

5. From the author's interview with a construction executive who worked on the new OWN headquarters in Los Angeles. Used with permission.

6. *Schindler's List*, directed by Steven Spielberg (1993; Hollywood, CA: Universal Studios, 1995), DVD.

7. David Nicolle, *The Mongol Warlords* (Leicester, UK: Brockhampton Press, 1998).

8. John of Plano Carpini, "History of the Mongols," *Mission to Asia*, ed. Christopher Dawson (Cambridge, MA: Medieval Academy of America, 1980), 29–30.

Chapter 6: The Engine of the Dove

1. "Immortality symbols" is a phrase used by author Dave Goetz throughout his great book *Death By Suburb* (New York: HarperCollins, 2006). He's referencing the things we cling to that make us feel like little gods—for example, when parents drive their kids to excel in a sport because it somehow makes them feel transcendent by extension.

2. G. K. Chesterton, *All Things Considered* (New York: John Lane Company, 1909), 53–54.

3. Frederica Mathewes-Green, "Gagging On Shiny, Happy People," *Christianity Today*, September 7, 1998, http://www.christianitytoday .com/ct/1998/september7/8ta092.html.

4. Jon Acuff, "Refusing to Take Compliments," JonAcuff.com, May 3, 2008, http://www.jonacuff.com/stuffchristianslike/2008/05/199-refus-ing-to-take-compliments/. Used with permission.

5. Bob Krulish's personal account of his dream. Used with permission.

6. Michael W. Smith, "Above All," *Worship* © 2001 Reunion.

7. Collin Hansen, "Passion Takes It Higher," *Christianity Today*, March 3, 2007, www.christianitytoday.com/ct/2007/april/20.29.html?start=2.

8. Mary Louise Kelly, "Saudi Princess Lobbies for Women's Right to Drive," *Morning Edition*, NPR, July 14, 2011, www.npr.org/2011/07/14 /137840538/saudi-princess-lobbies-for-womens-right-to-drive.

9. Eugene Peterson, *The Pastor: A Memoir* (New York: HarperOne, 2011), 247.

10. Hal Goble, interview with the author, November 13, 2010. Used with permission.

The Elegant Levers

1. *Aprecianado* is a word Tom Melton created to describe the marriage of "appreciation" and "aficianado"—and he embodies the word he created.

The Lever of Humility

1. Rachel Martin, "Should Gen. David Petraeus Have Five Stars?" *All Things Considered*, NPR, January 25, 2011, www.npr.org/2011/01/25/133218465 /Should-Gen-David-Petraeus-Have-Five-Stars.

2. Bob Greene, "4-Star General, 5-Star Grace," *CNN*, February 13, 2011, http://articles.cnn.com/2011-02-13/opinion/greene.gracious.gesture _1_chiarelli-karl-malone-pants?_s=PM:OPINION.

The Lever of Blunt

1. Christie Kelly, conversation with the author, May 2011. Used with permission.

2. Tamrat Layne, conversation with the author, March 2010. Used with

permission. Tamrat Layne has founded a ministry called Global Healing in Love and Unity (www.ghlu.org). His goal through the ministry, he says, is "transforming nations," and the focus is on Africa. Through GHLU, Layne aims to (1) reach out to leaders, (2) bring reconciliation among people groups and leaders, (3) be a catalyst for community transformation, and (4) equip a new generation for responsibilities in leadership and spiritual transformation.

3. Albert Mohler, "Doing Away With Hell? Part One," AlbertMohler.com, March 8, 2011, http://www.albertmohler.com/2011/03/08/doing-away-with-hell-part-one/.

The Lever of Beauty

1. Sara Groves, *Nomad* (2006; Provident Music Distribution), DVD.
2. Katha Pollitt, "What I Understood," *The Mind-Body Problem* (New York: Random House, 2009), 64.

The Lever of Pursuit

1. Email message to the author. Used with permission.
2. Used with permission.
3. Eric Westervelt, "Now Free, Some Czechs Fear Complacency," *Morning Edition*, NPR, November 11, 2009, http://www.npr.org/templates/transcript/transcript.php?storyId=120281482.

The Lever of Laughter

1. Eugene Peterson, *A Long Obedience In the Same Direction* (Downers Grove, IL: InterVarsity Press, 2000), 45.
2. Jonathan Kelly, email message to the author, July 2011. Used with permission.

3. Ed Rollins, "Commentary: Will 'SNL' Skit Sink Hopes for Obama?" *CNN*, October 7, 2009, http://articles.cnn.com/2009-10-07/politics /rollins.saturday.night.live.obama_1_snl-skit-president-obama -honeymoon?_s=PM:POLITICS.

4. Norman Solomon, *The Trouble with Dilbert* (Monroe, ME: Common Courage Press, 1997), page number unknown.

The Lever of Generosity

1. *Les Miserables*, directed by Bille August (Culver City, CA: Sony Pictures, 1998), DVD.

2. Bob Greene, "Frank Sinatra's Lesson In Loyalty," *CNN*, July 17, 2011, http://articles.cnn.com/2011-07-17/opinion/greene.sinatra.patsys_ 1_frank-sinatra-sinatra-legend-sinatra-story?_s=PM:OPINION.

3. JoAnn C. Jones, "Brockville," *Ontario-Guide Posts*, January 1996.

Astonish Me

1. "Romans: The Roman Army," *BBC*, http://www.bbc.co.uk/schools /primaryhistory/romans. The section on and detailed description of centurians no longer exists.